# FORMULA ONE
## THE CHAMPIONSHIP

# FORMULA ONE
## THE CHAMPIONSHIP

DAVID TREMAYNE

*A Complete Race by Race Guide*

*Photographs by Behram Kapadia*

‖ ·PARRAGON· ‖

First published in Great Britain in 1996 by
Parragon Book Service Ltd
Unit 13–17
Avonbridge Trading Estate
Atlantic Road
Avonmouth
Bristol BS11 9QD

ISBN: 0-75251-762-7

Conceived, designed and produced by Haldane Mason

***Acknowledgements***
Art Director: **Ron Samuels**
Editor: **Conan Nicholas**
Designer: **Robert Fairclough**

Colour reproduction by
Regent Publishing Services, Hong Kong

Printed in Italy

***Picture Acknowledgements***
All photographs by **Behram Kapadia** with the exception of
the following:
**L.A.T.:** back cover, 1, 2–3, 7, 10, 12–13, 14, 15, 16, 18, 20,
22, 23, 24, 25, 26, 30, 32, 33, 34, 35, 36, 37, 38, 39, 40, 41,
42, 43, 44, 45, 46–7, 63, 67, 68, 69 (top), 75, 76, 77 (bottom),
78, 90, 91 (top), 92 (bottom), 93 (top), 94, 95 (bottom);
**Autosport:** Front cover

# CONTENTS

# INTRODUCTION

THE PREMISES OF THE FEDERATION INTERNATIONALE DE L'AUTOMOBILE (FIA), WHICH governs world motorsport, are an impressive façade in an elegant part of Paris. But the real power bases in what traditionally used to be a sport run by the French, lie to the north of the English Channel. One lurks behind a nondescript frontage in London's Walton Street, barely a wind's breath of a green-and-gold carrier bag from Harrods in Knightsbridge. The other is behind the darkened glass and steel of a multi-storey residence in Kensington's Princes Gate.

These are the business premises of Max Mosley and Bernie Ecclestone respectively, the two powerbrokers who shape the future of Formula One (F1). Between them they effectively control the regulations of the sport, and the places where it is run. It has long been something of a running debate whether they get on like a house on fire, or like a house falling apart. When the mood takes them, either one can play the 'nice cop, nasty cop' routine to perfection. By appearing to divide themselves, they have frequently made their enemies fall.

Under their stewardship in recent years worldwide viewing figures have accelerated as quickly as the F1 cars themselves, coverage itself has been enhanced dramatically via the use of onboard cameras, and media interest in the sport has exceeded all previous bounds. At the same time more than 15 small teams – including some of the great names, such as Team Lotus – have gone to the wall, even though the FIA stemmed the increasingly complex and expensive technological development spiral in 1993. Critics of Mosley and Ecclestone say that, rather than doing anything significant to help such minnows survive, they have almost encouraged their decline. Both counter such accusations by pointing out that, when the kitchen gets too hot, it's best to remove oneself from the source of the heat, and that F1 owes nobody a living.

If the public face of the FIA is thus at times set, behind the scenes it has become a far-reaching animal. Law enforcement is now far tighter under the auspices of Technical Delegate Charlie Whiting, formerly chief mechanic when Ecclestone owned Brabham. And F1's medical arrangements are a lesson to all other sports as Professor Sid Watkins travels the world as Chief Medical Delegate. No face is more welcome to drivers awaiting treatment after accidents than the Prof's, which in favourable circumstances is usually decorated with a cigar and a craggy grin.

These are the hardened professionals who run Grand Prix racing today, and who have helped to make it what it is. It is a dictatorship, of course; against the intellectual cunning of the teams it has to be. But most of the time it is benign.

**Michael Schumacher** *slots himself into the driving seat as he prepares to take on all comers.*

# BERNIE ECCLESTONE

EVERYBODY IN MOTORSPORT KNOWS Bernie Ecclestone by name, but less is known about his antecedents. Bernie likes it that way. Being a closed book is often good for business. This is the man who was so offended by the sport's haphazard way of running itself in the early 1970s that he made it his (very profitable) business to change things. Via FOCA, the Formula One Constructors' Association, the majority of team owners have grown rich as their sport has prospered.

In his early days Ecclestone raced with some success at venues such as Brands Hatch, before acquiring the assets of the defunct Connaught Formula One team. He then moved on to manage drivers such as Stuart Lewis-Evans and 1970 champion Jochen Rindt, before buying Brabham and steering it towards World Championship success for Nelson Piquet in the early 1980s, but he was also the man who slew the

**Bernie Ecclestone** *is the man who has steered F1 to its current pre-eminent position.*

dragon of the old FIA and who, after a peaceful settlement to the infamous war between the Fédération Internationale du Sport Automobile (FISA) and FOCA, now acts as vice president of marketing for the latter, selling Grand Prix racing and its television rights across the globe.

A business magazine once listed him well up in the top 500 wealthiest people in sport. Max Mosley could not resist commenting: 'I think they may mistakenly have thought that Bernie's annual income was his overall wealth.' Ecclestone said nothing; not for nothing are his faxes wryly headed by the name 'Mr E' – 'mystery'.

Within Formula One it is well known that it is a good idea not to quarrel too much with him. He has said: 'I make a good friend but a bad enemy.'

Life is his poker game, and winning is everything, for at heart he remains what he has always been – a racer.

# MAX MOSLEY

URBANITY, YOUTHFUL LOOKS, A WRY sense of humour and the self-confessed 'ability to appear to be a gentleman while being completely self-serving' are character traits that have stood Max Mosley well in his path to the presidency of the FIA. You might throw in controversy, too, for this is the son of Sir Oswald Mosley, who was interned in the Second World War for espousing the cause of Adolf Hitler.

Born into wealth (his mother Diana Guinness, interned in Holloway during his wartime birth, is one of the Mitford sisters), he studied law, which was useful when he came to finance his aspirations as a racing driver. He began in club racing before vaulting on to the international stage by competing in Formula Two. He was at Hockenheim in the race in which Clark was killed.

Mosley cheerfully admits that his true talents lay in other directions, specifically management and finance. He employed

**Max Mosley** *has proved an able politician since he took over presidency of the FIA.*

these to the maximum when he helped designer Robin Herd found March Engineering. Typically, they leaped straight into building not only minor-league racing cars, but also F1 in a grandiose style never seen before or since. Later, he acted as FOCA's lawyer in the acrimonious fight with Jean-Marie Balestre at the FIA and its sporting branch, FISA. And it was Balestre whom Mosley deposed in October 1991 to take over the reins of the sport.

Since then he has coped admirably with the fall-out of the Imola tragedies, and steered the sport towards a position compatible with the likely environmental requirements of the foreseeable future. The FIA now has active roles not only in roadcar safety testing, but in many areas of interest to the general public. Suggest that his presidency may be a valuable springboard to a political career within the European Parliament, and he does not demur.

With **Michael Schumacher,** *Ferrari's Prancing Horse has a reigning World Champion at the helm for the first time since 1990.*

# FRANK WILLIAMS

IN F1 ONLY WINNERS SURVIVE, AND against all odds Frank Williams has survived longer than most. In the earliest days his team was little more than a joke as he struggled to keep it afloat in a hand-to-mouth existence that militated against progress, but the mark of this man is his ability to fight adversity and never to give up. He fought back when he lost control of his team in 1976, and again 10 years later when his own driving error resulted in a road accident in which he was paralysed. Frank took full responsibility for his own situation, and never looked back. When he reappeared on the F1 scene at the British Grand Prix that July, he received an impromptu ovation.

When the mood takes him he can be wily and awkward, but Frank Williams has a nose for racing and a determination quite beyond the understanding of most observers. His race team is everything to him, and this dedicated racer is justly proud of its Championship-winning engineering excellence, which frequently sets the standard.

# RON DENNIS

WHEN RON DENNIS AND DESIGN guru John Barnard were brought into McLaren at the end of 1980, the famous British team was virtually on its knees. Within a year their blend of management and technology had won them their first Grand Prix; within four years they were champions of the world. They stayed at or near the top for the following nine years.

Along the way Dennis's unusual style made a casualty of Barnard, who moved to Ferrari, but McLaren continued to prosper under the guidance of a man who had started out working as a mechanic for Cooper back in the 1960s and worked himself steadily through a succession of roles until he knew the score thoroughly.

A sensitive fellow behind an outwardly arrogant appearance, Dennis doesn't like to be reminded too often of this, yet it undoubtedly laid the foundations that allowed him to create one of the most successful racing teams in history. Observers now wait to see if this remarkable manager can steer McLaren back to its old form after a series of disappointing performances during 1995.

**Michael Schumacher and Monaco:** *The former is reigning World Champion, the latter the most famous jewel in Formula One's crown.*

# FLAVIO BRIATORE

WHO IS FLAVIO BRIATORE? THE FOCUS of television cameras as Benetton wins races, Briatore is familiar as the bronzed Italian with the back-turned cap, who came into Benetton in 1989 and stirred everything up. Yet prior to that his antecedents are more mysterious than those of the Lone Ranger.

Benetton says he was working in its New York offices when he got the call to sort out the F1 team, and he wasted little time in breaking eggs to make a fresh omelette. Out went manager Peter Collins and his protégé Johnny Herbert. Later came Michael Schumacher. The F1 world sat up. Briatore made things happen.

In 1994 Schumacher won the Drivers' World Championship amid a flood of controversy that Briatore shrugged off. He had set himself the goal of championship success, suggesting he might seek something else to do if he failed. Last year it was repeated, with the added bonus of Benetton's first Constructors' title. Primarily a businessman and not, like rivals, a racer, Briatore remains an enigma.

# LUCA DI MONTEZEMOLO

WHEN, IN 1975, NIKI LAUDA FINALLY realized the promise he had shown all through 1974 and took his Ferrari to the Drivers' and Constructors' World Championships by a healthy margin, a young aristocratic Roman stood quietly in the background. This was Luca di Montezemolo, a trained lawyer who had been installed by Enzo Ferrari himself the previous season to shake up a Ferrari F1 team that had slumped to shambolic ineptitude in 1973. Di Montezemolo steadily rebuilt the great race team, before his talents were required elsewhere within the mighty Fiat empire. Italy's football World Cup beckoned.

Ferrari, meanwhile, collapsed again in 1991 amid a welter of inter-team acrimony. Drastic surgery was required, and as Lauda came back to act as consultant to his old team, di Montezemolo was installed as president of the sport's greatest team. Just as in 1975, results are expected – and to produce them, di Montezemolo has secured the services of Michael Schumacher.

# EDDIE JORDAN

OF ALL THE MANY TEAM OWNERS WHO have optimistically set their cap at F1 success in the past decade, only the mercurial Edmund Jordan has achieved his aims, and as things fall into perspective with the passing of the years since his graduation to what Ron Dennis calls 'The Piranha Club' in 1991, it is possible to see just what a good job he has done. Others have concentrated too much on engineering, or fallen into the trap of having to take on a sponsor as a partner, only to lose control of everything they have worked so hard to create. But Jordan has assessed the financial needs of an F1 team, and taken care of business.

Within the sport this colourful individual has a reputation for blunt talk, expressed in jocular terms. His vocabulary might offend visiting nuns, and his will-o'-the-wisp nature frequently frustrates those who believe that they desperately need to speak with him. But through not just F1 paddocks, but motor-racing paddocks all over the globe, Jordan knows everyone. And everyone knows him. Now he needs that first F1 victory. Be sure, it will come.

# THE CIRCUITS

INTEREST IN THE GLAMOROUS WORLD OF FORMULA ONE Grand Prix motor racing has never been higher, even though most of the financial capitals around the globe have only just begun staggering out of the debilitating recession of the 1980s. If you believe what FIA president Max Mosley and vice president of marketing Bernie Ecclestone tell you, they receive requests every week of the year from somebody, somewhere, seeking to run a Grand Prix. Some, like that colourful builder/enthusiast/museum-owner Tom Wheatcroft, who owns the Donington Park track in the UK, thus fulfilled a lifetime dream.

There is no question. Today's tobacco-funded, manufacturer-supported, rubber-burning, candy-coloured kaleidoscope of open-wheeled chariot racing is playing to packed audiences.

The 1996 schedule takes in 14 countries, starting in Australia, then moving almost as rapidly as the cars themselves to Brazil, Argentina, Germany, Italy, Monte Carlo, Spain, Canada, France, Britain, Germany again, Hungary, Belgium, Italy again, Portugal and, finally, Japan. It is a whirlwind tour that barely breaks its stride: 16 Grand Prix races are packed into eight all-action months, with barely more than two-week breaks between each contest. And the moment it is over, the teams will begin planning and working towards the next in a never-ceasing schedule of designing, building and testing. There is no such thing as a closed season these days. And there are other nations awaiting their chance. In recent years there has been continued interest from North America (despite the strong domestic championships for open-wheeled IndyCars and NASCAR stock cars), Indonesia, China and Russia.

What is the attraction? It isn't simply a matter of the size of the paying-gate on the day, for even at the best venues that barely rates higher than 200,000 people over three or four days. Indeed, the final Australian Grand Prix in Adelaide in 1995 set the recognized record, at 205,000.

The value goes far deeper than that, for an established place in the Grand Prix community says so much not just for a nation's sporting pretensions but, much more seriously, it allows it to participate in a mega-buck business that is recognized the world over. People invest in Grand Prix racing because it works. Television viewing figures have been skyrocketing in the past five years, and that is great news for companies seeking a medium in which to put across their corporate message to existing and potential clients across the globe. On the following pages we plot the geographical progress of the 1996 FIA Formula One World Championship. All 16 venues are outlined in detail and their salient points of topography and historical interest are analysed – from the glamour of Monte Carlo's streets to the chill of Hockenheim's tall pines, from the challenge of Belgium's Spa-Francorchamps, to the controversial tarmac of Japan's Suzuka Circuit.

**Multi-hues and multi-millions:** *Formula One motor racing is currently one of the few global sports that is increasing its market.*

# AUSTRALIAN GRAND PRIX

## Albert Park, Melbourne

**A**USTRALIA JOINED THE GRAND PRIX circus in 1985, when drivers first took to the streets of Adelaide in a race that concluded the season. Keke Rosberg's dominant victory for Williams set the seal on Adelaide's future, and until 1995 the Thunder Down Under or Sensational Adelaide – as it was frequently billed – proved the most popular event on the calendar. Whether this was simply because it was the final race of the year and more often than not had an end-of-term atmosphere because the World Championship had been settled, is a moot point. The South Australians tackled their racing with enthusiasm and efficiency, and the City of Churches track was, unusually, very quick for a street venue.

Though Adelaide only truly settled the outcome of the title fight twice – in 1986 and 1994 – it threw up many unforgettable moments, none more exciting than the high-speed puncture on the Brabham Straight that robbed Nigel Mansell of the Championship in 1986, just when his comfortable second place behind team-mate

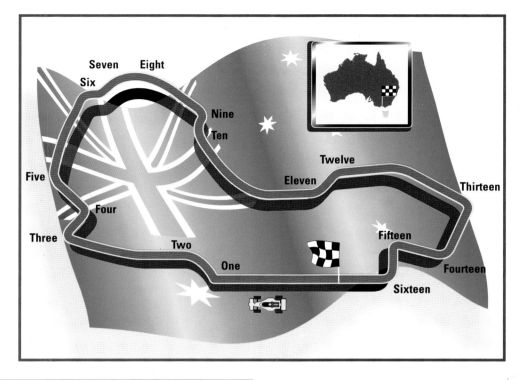

mer event, in particular when Nelson Piquet was unable to see Piercarlo Ghinzani's Osella in front of him on the main straight and scooped under the back of it, and Ayrton Senna later took a front wheel off his leading McLaren when he was unable to see Martin Brundle's Brabham immediately ahead in the appalling gloom. Despite that, the only serious injury sustained there came in 1995 when Mika Hakkinen was hospitalized after crashing heavily following a sudden puncture on his McLaren. Happily, the Finn has recovered fully.

Adelaide survived everything until financial and political circumstances militated against it. Then, early in 1995 a superior bid was made by the state of Victoria, which sought yet another of the world's glittering sports prizes for its capital Melbourne to add to the annual frenzy of that most famous horse-race, the Melbourne Cup. While the South Australians were left to realize, too late in some cases, just what they had lost, the Victorians won the right to stage the prestigious race from 1996, albeit at a price. Plans to hold the race in picturesque Albert Park – which had hosted races back in the 1950s – met with ferocious opposition from well-organized protest groups that even went so far as to fly to London in an unsuccessful effort to lobby FIA marketing supremo Bernie Ecclestone. Even hardened race fans expressed the view that Albert Park was simply too scenic a venue for F1, and that another street circuit might have been more sensible.

There were suggestions that protesters would try to disrupt the final Adelaide race – they came to nothing, but the teams went to Melbourne for the first race of 1996 prepared to face the worst. As they did so, many harboured memories of dramatic outbraking battles at the end of the Brabham Straight, or of the Foster's party on the Wednesday preceding the race, where snakes would be draped around the shoulders of trembling guests. Melbourne had an awful lot to live up to.

**As F1 moved to Melbourne,** *many still held happy memories of Adelaide, where Hill won in 1995 (left) as Frentzen and Herbert (lapping Blundell, inset) fought for second place.*

Nelson Piquet and ahead of Alain Prost guaranteed him the crown. That heartache was flashed all around the globe, as was the Briton's anguished expression on the long walk home. History repeated itself when his spiritual successor at Williams, Damon Hill, clashed violently with Michael Schumacher at the end of the tragic 1994 season.

Twice the race was cut short by torrential rain, in 1989 and 1991. It was a long way to go for mere handfuls of laps, and there was a fierce outcry against the for-

## NEW CIRCUIT

**CIRCUIT LENGTH:** 5.26 km (3.26 miles)
**LOCATION:** Albert Park, 220 Albert Road, South Melbourne. 3 km (2 miles) south of Melbourne city centre. Tel: 613 9258 7100.
**RACE DISTANCE:** 58 laps
**1995 POLE POSITION:** Hill 1 m 15.505 s (Adelaide)
**1995 WINNER:** Hill 1 h 49 m 15.946 s (Adelaide)
**1995 FASTEST LAP:** Hill 1 m 17.943 s (Adelaide)

AUSTRALIA

# BRAZILIAN GRAND PRIX

**Autodromo Jose Carlos Pace, Interlagos, São Paulo** **March 31**

**B**ACK IN THE REALLY GOOD OLD DAYS, Interlagos was one of the most truly majestic of all Grand Prix circuits, pitching drivers straight into an awesomely fast banked left-hand curve immediately after the start which seemed to go on forever and really sorted the Coulds from the Thought They Coulds.

That was in the 1970s when the circuit played regular host to the Brazilian Grand Prix in the heyday of Emerson Fittipaldi, the country's first World Champion, and Carlos Pace, who won in 1975 and in whose honour the circuit is now named.

But then came the threat from the Jacarepagua track in Rio de Janeiro, which held the race in 1978, and then won the rights to it from 1981 and held it right through to 1989.

That year massive changes were made to the old track in the home town of Ayrton Senna. From its original 7 km (4.3 miles) it was cut down to a more manageable 4.3 km (2.7 miles). The new track made use of existing surface within the old, cleverly weaving them together to create something new which, while not as exciting or demanding, neverthe-

less retained the old track's immense character. At the same time other facilities were improved, and when the race came back to Interlacos for 1990 it did so for good.

Interlagos places great strain on transmissions, and the long, long left-hander that leads into the final stages of the lap can be exhausting even for the fittest drivers. In 1994 Senna's discomfort in the cramped cockpit of his Williams-Renault finally caught him cut in his great fight with Schumacher, making him spin from second place at the Junçao corner.

1993 monsoon as he tried to avoid Christian Fittipaldi's Minardi.

The Brazilian Grand Prix has sometimes been the opening round of the Championship. On the occasions when it has not, it has been the venue where those teams who were competitive first time out seek to confirm the results of the first race, and those who were struggling look for inspiration and for more optimistic pointers to their form over the rest of the season. If you go well at Interlagos, with its variety of corners, it is a good augury. If you are viewing there, the walk out to the Subida do Lago corner at the end of the back straight is taxing but rewarding, as this is where the cars start braking from their maximum speed, while those less inclined towards exercise may satisfy themselves with the drop at the end of the pits. This is especially exciting at the start, as those who witnessed the tangle between Berger and Andretti in 1993 will recall. This is a slower section, so you can see the drivers working hard. Alternatively, the climb from Junçao through Subida dos Boxes and on to Arquibancadas gives an excellent chance to get close to F1 cars as they accelerate up to their maximum speed. You may have to watch what you eat and drink very carefully at Interlagos, but it's a great place to watch racing cars in action!

**Oops!** *As Hakkinen leads Berger, Herbert and Alesi in pursuit of the leaders at the start of the 1995 race, the unfortunate Panis heads for collision with the wall on the tricky first corner.*

**CIRCUIT LENGTH:** 4.325 km (2.684 miles)
**LOCATION:** Avenida Senador Teotonio Vilela, 261, 01000 000 São Paulo, 16 km (10 miles) south of the centre of São Paulo. Tel: 55 11 521 9911/521 9832
**RACE DISTANCE:** 71 laps
**1995 POLE POSITION:** Hill 1 m 20.081 s
**1995 WINNER:** Schumacher 1 h 38 m 34.154 s
**1995 FASTEST LAP:** Schumacher 1 m 20.921 s

From the start/finish line drivers file through the tight downhill drop to the left at the end of the pit block before twitching right and then curving into a long left-hander that leads to the sixth-gear back straight, where Irvine, Verstappen, Brundle and Eric Bernard were involved in the spectacular collision in the 1994 race that saw Irvine banned for three races. At the end of that two left-handers lead to the fourth-gear right, Feradura, that signals the start of the twisting infield section, which includes a second-gear hairpin, that leads to the third-gear Junçao. This is a tightening left-hander that sets them up for the run to the finish line, where Alain Prost lost control of his Williams, aquaplaning into a spin, in the

# ARGENTINIAN GRAND PRIX

## Autodromo Oscar Alfredo Galvez, Parc Almirante Brown, Buenos Aires

IN THE HALCYON DAYS OF THE EARLY 1970s, when the Argentinian Grand Prix was a regular fixture in the F1 calendar, the two South American races kicked off the season in January and February, before a rest period prior to the South African Grand Prix in March.

Now the season has become more compressed and, if the 1995 Argentinian race is anything to go by, that's an unfortunate development because the early April date put it firmly into the onset of Argentina's winter. Consequently the principal memories the F1 corps entertained of that race were of rain – barely a day of the meeting was not wet at some stage, with consequent severe flooding of access roads – and disappointment at the way in which this circuit had been modified to make it suitable for the 1990s.

In common with Interlagos, the Autodromo Oscar Alfredo Galvez at Parc Almirante Brown is a pale shadow of its former self. When local hero Carlos Reutemann caused a sensation in 1972 by planting his Brabham on pole position on his first Grand Prix appearance, it was a steely place that sent cars into a left/right flick called Tobogán at the end of the pit straight, into a looping 180-degree right-hander called Horquilla, through another gentle left and then on to a back straight that went on forever until the Curvon bend eased right through 200 degrees and led everyone on to a shorter straight prior to a 90-degree right. There followed a right-hand hairpin and a series of wiggles that were reminiscent of the track in Mexico City, before two tight left-handers completed the lap. Now the circuit is scarcely recognizable. From the revised start/finish line it's a short blast to Curva Numero Uno, a very tight right-hander which comes back on itself prior to the 180-degree left-hander, Confiteria, which

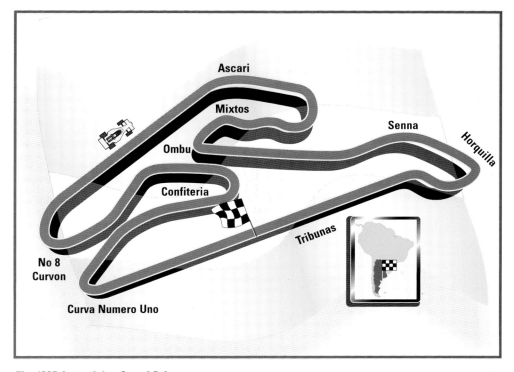

**CIRCUIT LENGTH:** 4.259 km (2.640 miles)
**LOCATION:** Av. General Paz y Av. Julio A. Roca, 1439 Buenos Aires, between downtown Buenos Aires and the Ezeiza International Airport. Tel: 54 1 638 1995 to 1999
**RACE DISTANCE:** 72 laps
**1995 POLE POSITION:** Coulthard 1 m 53.241 s
**1995 WINNER:** Hill 1 h 53 m 14.532 s
**1995 FASTEST LAP:** Schumacher 1 m 30.52 s

**The 1995 Argentinian Grand Prix** *gave an accurate preview of the season as Schumacher fought Hill.*

then leads to a left/right dogleg and another 180-degree hairpin, this time to the right. There it feeds on to the second longest straight, which arcs right through Ascari until two 90-degree right-handers lead drivers through a series of S-bends to Mixtos, the very sharp left-hander that used to signal the end of the lap. Now they continue down a shortened version of the old pit straight to the wiggle of Senna (the former Tobogán) and the two 90-degree rights at Horquilla, and the final 90-degree left that brings them back to the pit straight.

Jackie Stewart won that 1972 race at 161.46 kmh (100.33 mph); Damon Hill won last year's damp race at 162.37 kmh (100.89 mph). Such may be the price of progress. Reutemann himself was present, and for the first time since his retirement from the sport in 1982 drove an F1 car. In a Ferrari 412T2 he was sensationally accomplished. Now the Governor of Santa Fé, he more than any rued the changes to the circuit, but spoke optimistically of a return to the older layout if sufficient finance can be raised.

If the current circuit lacks charisma, Buenos Aires itself is redolent with it, and is packed with restaurants which serve the tremendous steaks for which the country is famous. It's a long way to go, especially if the weather is inclement, but for a glimpse at a totally different culture it's a fascinating event to attend. Why is the circuit named after local hero Oscar Alfredo Galvez rather than the late Juan Manuel Fangio? That's anyone's guess.

# EUROPEAN GRAND PRIX

## Nurburgring

**W**HEN THE F1 WORLD WENT BACK to the 'new' Nurburgring in chilly October last year for the European Grand Prix, it was pleasantly surprised. What it had collectively remembered from its last visit as a sterile, unimaginative little track turned out to be not so bad after all, which just goes to show that 10 years can be an very long time in motorsport.

Just as Hockenheim, Zolder and Imola have stigmas to bear for the rest of their days, so the new Nurburgring will forever suffer from comparison with the old. This is located very close to the current track, and nestles menacingly in the Adenau Forest, a great Everest of a track, 22.7 km (14.1 miles) of twisting, turning, taxing road that winds and sweeps and plunges its way through and round the environs of the old Nurburg Castle, a majestic circuit to end all circuits, upon which some of the greatest Grands Prix in history had been staged.

Here, at the old 'Ring in 1938, Britain's ill-fated pre-war star Dick Seaman had won his first Grand Prix for Mercedes-Benz as he struggled with the increasingly embarrassing situation of being an Englishman in a Nazi-sponsored team. Here in 1957 'old man' Fangio had dished out the beating of their lives to gay young

blades Mike Hawthorn and Peter Collins, as he drove the race of his career to overcome their Ferrari after his Maserati had established an early lead only to lose it, and a lot more, during a traumatic pit stop. Here four years later Stirling Moss used his mastery and the handling of his underpowered Lotus to trounce the more powerful but less wieldy Ferraris, and seven years later still

**Memories of the 'new' Nurburgring** *were anything but favourable, following two lukewarm Grands Prix there in 1984 and 1985, and few F1 observers had a good word for the track that had supplanted the legendary 'old' 'Ring. But the 1995 European Grand Prix proved a popular success, indicating how much times have changed in a decade of racing.*

**CIRCUIT LENGTH:** 4.542 km (2.822 miles)
**LOCATION:** Nurburgring GmbH, 53520 Nurburg. 70 km (43.5 miles) south of Köln on A1-E29, or 60 km (37 miles) west of Koblenz on A48-E44 to Koblenz and then A61 until Wehr/ Nurburgring exit.
Tel: 49 2 691 3020
**RACE DISTANCE:** 68 laps
**1995 POLE POSITION:** Coulthard 1 m 18.738 s
**1995 WINNER:** Schumacher 1 h 39 m 59.044 s
**1995 FASTEST LAP:** Schumacher 1 m 21.180 s

Jackie Stewart somehow saw the way round in the murk and fog to win by the astonishing margin of four minutes in a race that should never have been started. Yet it was also at the old 'Ring that Niki Lauda had his fiery accident, and while it failed to claim the life he appeared to have lost, it was the end for the circuit as a Grand Prix venue. It was just too long to be marshalled with the levels of efficiency the sport now demanded.

Inevitably the new Nurburgring was going to fare badly in any comparison, and races in 1984 and 1985 came and went without favourable comment. The German Grand Prix moved home permanently to Hockenheim. Yet last year the 'Ring came to be viewed in a different light, for by modern standards it was a reasonable place, the European Grand Prix rendered all the more exciting because of a damp track surface.

The Castrol-S curve caused some fun at the start, while the off-camber Ford-Kurve that follows and, even more so, the hairpin Dunlop-Kurve and the ensuing sweeps to Bit-Kurve, provided plenty of side-by-side motor racing in the conditions, though the Veedol-Schikane sadly emasculated the one really quick part on the back of the course.

With its 12 corners and curves packed compactly into 4.5 km (2.8 miles), the new Nurburgring is one of those circuits where spectators can see a lot for their Deutschmarks, and the section from the Ford-Kurve to Bit-Kurve is a natural amphitheatre. If you're going to the Nurburgring race and you take a camera, opportunities are reasonably good, and should be better now that the race takes place in April rather than October when snow is on the hills and sometimes lower than that. Be sure to visit the museum in the circuit grounds just by the main gate (remembering that it does not take credit cards!). But, most of all, get there early enough to treat yourself to some laps of the old 'Ring, which help you appreciate what sort of challenge motor racing used to throw down.

EUROPE

# SAN MARINO GRAND PRIX

**Autodromo Enzo e Dino Ferrari, Imola**

PRIOR TO THE TRAGIC EVENTS OF 1994, the Autodromo at Imola named after the late Enzo Ferrari and his ill-starred son Dino had a reputation as one of the most demanding yet popular tracks in the F1 schedule. A circuit where power still counted despite a rash of little chicanes that had blemished its original simplicity, it often heralded the start of the European season and was the venue where many teams felt that the Championship really began. Teams that had got off to good starts in South or North America, Japan or South Africa,

depending on the exact make-up of the calendar, had usually tested since the first races and honed their packages. Others, who had met adversity or whose cars were not quite up to the mark, had been able to make improvements.

This was the precise situation in 1994, when Benetton arrived in Imola having won the opening races in Brazil and Aida, near Kobe in Japan, and Williams produced aerodynamic modifications that it hoped would rectify the shortcomings its FW16s had displayed in each of them. As history relates, that weekend brought

back the spectre of death to F1 for the first time since Elio de Angelis died testing a Brabham at Paul Ricard in 1986. The weekend began badly when Rubens Barrichello escaped a very heavy accident in his Jordan on the Friday. Then newcomer Roland Ratzenberger was killed at the Villeneuve corner in qualifying on Saturday afternoon after sustaining damage to a front wing earlier in the lap. As the teams came to terms with two body blows, Senna died on the seventh lap of the race after a huge accident in the Tamburello corner after the pits. Motor

**CIRCUIT LENGTH:** 5.040 km (3.132 miles)
**LOCATION:** S.A.G.I.S. SpA, Via Fratelli Rosselli, 2, 4006 Imola (BO). 33 km (20.5 miles) south-east of Bologna on A14 or SS9.
Tel: 39 542 31444
**RACE DISTANCE:** 63 laps
**1995 POLE POSITION:** Schumacher 1 m 27.274 s
**1995 WINNER:** Hill 1 h 41 m 42.552 s
**1995 FASTEST LAP:** Berger 1 m 29.568 s

racing was plunged into the same sort of critical self-examination and total perplexity that had followed the death of Jim Clark at Hockenheim 26 years earlier, and the changes that would emanate from Imola that weekend were indeed far-reaching, for the political climate had changed considerably since the 1960s and Senna's demise had been that rare (and therefore even more shocking) thing: a sportsman's death televised live.

In the past there had been many accidents at Tamburello: Piquet in 1987; Berger in the fire of 1989; Alboreto in 1991; Patrese in 1992. Yet each time the driver had survived.

Until 1994, drivers went flat through Tamburello, an ongoing left-hander which led to the fast straight which swept right through Villeneuve before the left-hand Tosa hairpin, then on up the climb to Piratella, and down again into the plunge to the Acque Minerali chicane and another climb to the highest part of the course and the Variante Alta dogleg. From there this spectacularly scenic track plunged back downhill to the twin left-handers called Rivazza, and towards the pits via the Variante Bassa chicane and then the sharp left/right complex of Traguardo which led on to the pit straight. The chicanes apart, it was a throwback to the original layout of the late 1940s.

Now Tamburello, like Senna, has gone, replaced by a left and a right and another left to slow things down, and Villeneuve has likewise been bypassed. To even things out a little, Acque Minerali is no longer a silly chicane, and Rivazza has greater run-off area.

Imola is no longer what it used to be physically, but spiritually it remains one of the great places to enjoy motorsport, in an atmosphere where the Italian fans – the *tifosi* – add a great new dimension.

**The Imola circuit will** *always be remembered as the place where Senna died, but it also deserves to be thought of as a spiritual home of the sport. The 1995 race (above left) started on a damp track, but nevertheless proved a cathartic success.*

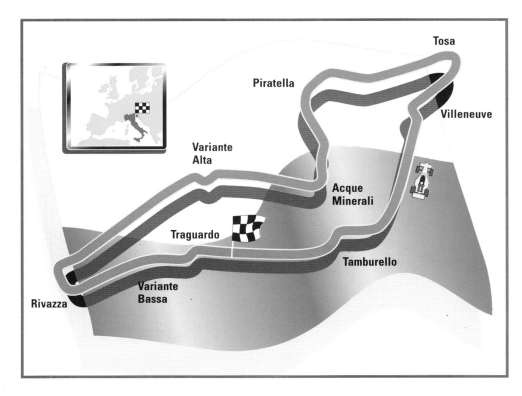

Tosa

Piratella

Villeneuve

Variante Alta

Acque Minerali

Traguardo

Tamburello

Rivazza

Variante Bassa

SAN MARINO

# MONACO GRAND PRIX

## Monte Carlo

ASK ANYBODY IN THE STREET TO name one Grand Prix, and it is likely that they would respond with Monaco. One of the oldest-established events in the motor racing calendar, it is surely the most charismatic, even if it is a fact that life in the Principality, for both racers and race-goers, is not all a bed of roses.

Monaco is part of the fabric of motorsport. Though overtaking is almost impossible, the charm and paradox of the place is enough, and the races over the years have invariably written some of the great legends. Graham Hill's five wins; Ayrton Senna's six; Villeneuve dashing past Jones in 1981 – all have taken their

place in the history books. For photographers Monaco is a wonderful place, as it offers so many different opportunities provided you have the right ticket. The architecture itself is spectacular, and so are the changes in elevation all round the circuit and the view across the harbour.

Getting to Monaco is an easy enough flight to Nice and cab to Monte Carlo itself, but be prepared to spend, spend, spend. Accommodation is very expensive, particularly with the 'extra' day engineered into the schedule between practices, and so is food. Be sure to book restaurants in advance, rather than shopping around and discovering that the

**CIRCUIT LENGTH:** 3.328 km (2.087 miles)
**LOCATION:** 3 Boulevard Albert 1ᵉ, BP 464, 98012 Monaco Cedex.18 km (11 miles) east of Nice via the A8-E80 or RN7. Tel: 33 93 15 2600
**RACE DISTANCE:** 78 laps
**1995 POLE POSITION:** Hill 1 m 21.952 s
**1995 WINNER:** Schumacher 1 l 53 m 11.258 s
**1995 FASTEST LAP:** Alesi 1 m 24.621 s

world and his wife are already there before you. If the hustle and bustle is what you want, fine, and make sure you go along to the Tip Top bar down the hill from Casino Square if you want to see some racing personalities. Most of the time it's

aren't so elevated, and getting the train in to the station in Monaco.

Quite the greatest thing about Monaco is how close you can get to cars travelling at ridiculous speeds. Television cameras can foreshorten the action, and at normal tracks distance can rob the spectacle of some of its speed, but at Monaco the confined nature of the circuit, with its walls and Armco barriers, somehow exaggerates it. If you are lucky enough to get a pass to walk through the tunnel, do so; it is quite the most terrifying thing to do when the cars are running by at 270 kmh (168 mph), but also the most exhilarating. If nothing else, a trip to Monaco always sends you home with a fresh respect for the abilities of the men who drive the cars, not to mention those who design them to achieve a level of performance your eyes and brain tell you is impossible.

Even if you can't get passes, there are some great spectating areas. It's probably better to avoid La Rascasse if you want to see something more than F1 cars burbling slowly, but somewhere like the Swimming Pool (Piscine) grandstands gives an excellent chance to see cars coming from Tabac, and to take in the breathtaking speed with which they change direction and pound on towards the second part of the Pool chicane.

**Brilliant scenery** *and a narrow street circuit lends the Monaco Grand Prix an aura all its own. Above, Eddie Irvine exits Casino Square; below, the very quick section round the swimming pool.*

mechanics and journalists imbibing and swapping tales, but if you pick the night before the free day you may be lucky enough to spot a Gerhard Berger, or a non-racing celebrity, socializing. Also, be prepared for tackling a lot of steps!

If you prefer the quiet, less energetic life, you might consider staying a little further down the coast, where the prices

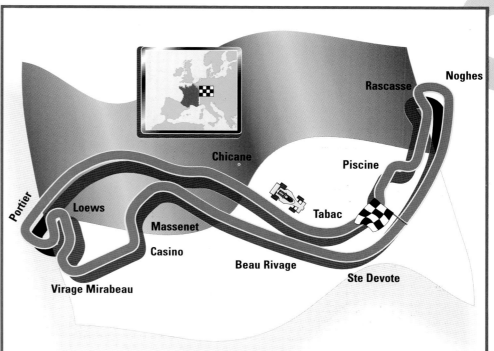

Noghes

Rascasse

Chicane

Piscine

Portier

Loews

Tabac

Massenet

Casino

Beau Rivage

Virage Mirabeau

Ste Devote

# SPANISH GRAND PRIX

## Circuit di Catalunya, Barcelona

**W**HAT MOTOR RACING FAN CAN ever forget the sight of Nigel Mansell and Ayrton Senna running wheel-to-wheel down the pit straight, mere inches apart at 290 kmh (180 mph)? This is the very essence of automobile competition – two cars side by side, each at maximum speed, their drivers straining everything and using every psychological trick short of weaving at each other – and in 1991 it was made possible in a gripping Spanish Grand Prix duel between the Williams and McLaren team leaders by the length of the pit straight of the Circuit di Catalunya, near Barcelona, and the very quick corner that leads on to it.

The Spanish Grand Prix has had many homes over the years, ranging in recent times from the sterility of Jarama, to the awesome but now sadly unused Montjuich Park, and the lonely Jerez where the F1 circus is almost on first-name terms with the crowd, and where Martin Donnelly was so fortunate to survive his massive accident in 1990. But now it seems to have established a comfortable new home at Barcelona, where it first moved in 1991.

This purpose-built facility incorporates the very latest facilities for teams

**CIRCUIT LENGTH:** 4.747 km (2.949 miles)
**LOCATION:** Carretera de Granollers, km 2, Montmelo, Barcelona. 20 km (12.5 miles) north of Barcelona, 80 km (50 miles) south of Girona. Tel: 00 34 35719700
**RACE DISTANCE:** 65 laps
**1995 POLE POSITION:** Schumacher 1 m 21.452 s
**1995 WINNER:** Schumacher 1 h 34 m 20.507 s
**1995 FASTEST LAP:** Hill 1 m 24.531 s

**The field bunched** *in the very first corner in 1995 (left), but Schumacher (right) won easily.*

and media, allied to a track layout that includes a wide variety of corners. The sloping pit straight ends in a 90-degree right-hand bend called Elf, which almost immediately gives way to a climbing left which opens out into a sweeping 180-degree right-hander followed very quickly by a second called Repsol. After a short straight the tight Seat left-hander

drops cars downhill through two further lefts and a gentle right at Wuth, then the track leads to the Campsa right-hander which takes drivers on to the back straight. Here the Nissan chicane slows them slightly in the run to the 180-degree left-hand hairpin called La Caixa, which then climbs gently through a 180-degree right into the two final 100-degree bends

which lead the cars at high speed back on to the straight.

The Circuit di Catalunya is very like Estoril in layout and feel, but with more run-off areas and a markedly smoother surface. It is popular with drivers, with its variety of second-gear to fast fourth/fifth-gear corners, although like Estoril its best overtaking opportunity lies on that 322 kmh (200 mph) straight, as Mansell will testify. Here the art of setting up a car lies in trading off the downforce that will yield good speed through the fast and slow corners, with the need to have as little drag as possible for maximum speed down the straight.

Besides that unforgettable 1991 race, Barcelona has also seen other great events, such as the 1992 Grand Prix when Michael Schumacher underlined his potential by finishing a stylish second in the rain to the unstoppable Mansell despite a heavy accident in qualifying. The 1993 race nearly saw Damon Hill win for the first time until he hit trouble with his Williams and victory went to cramped team-mate Alain Prost, while 1994 was the occasion when Schumacher nursed his car home a brilliant second even though it was stuck in fifth gear.

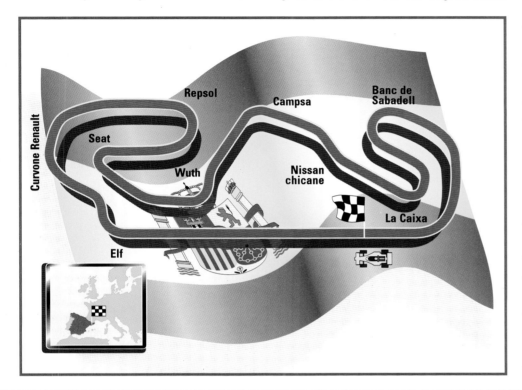

# CANADIAN GRAND PRIX

## Circuit Gilles Villeneuve, Montreal

THE CIRCUIT GILLES VILLENEUVE IN Montreal provides few opportunities for overtaking, but is still a great place to watch racing cars. Though it looks like one, it is not a permanent facility. Backing on to the old Olympic Rowing Basin near the 1967 Expo Pavilion, on a site on the cold St Lawrence River, it is put together like Adelaide in time for the Grand Prix each June. There are always plenty of spectators, and now that Jacques Villeneuve has moved from IndyCars to F1,

**The Ferrari pit** *explodes (right) as Alesi wins.*

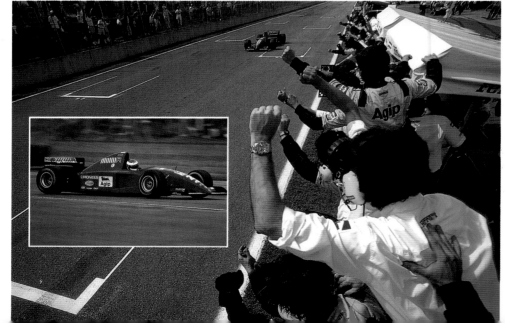

the gates will be flooded with even more fans waving the Maple Leaf this year.

Montreal may lack the appeal of the old Mosport Park which was once home to the Canadian race, but it is still an imposing track. The sweep past the pits and through a gentle right-hand arc before very heavy braking for the first, tight left-hander, is spine-tingling, and the bunching in that first corner usually compromises somebody's race. That left leads into a 180-degree right that climbs uphill and funnels cars through an arcing right to the first very tight left/right chicane, before another burst of speed on the curving back straight winds them down to the hairpin where Mika Hakkinen assaulted Johnny Herbert – to their mutual detriment – in last year's event. The beginning of this stretch, from the chicane, is out of bounds, bordered by parkland on the infield and the St Lawrence on the outside, but you can watch closer to the hairpin, which is often a good site for overtaking attempts. Out of the hairpin drivers accelerate hard past the site where the pits used to be located, but now a makeshift chicane has

**The Canadians** *applaud Alesi's triumph (left).*

spoiled what used to be the daunting plunge at maximum speed along the lip of the Rowing Basin and down to Casino Bend, the second real chicane. This is, nevertheless, still a good spectating spot. From there it's another blast before the two tight 90-degree flicks that end the lap, one to the right, the other to the left and on to the pit straight.

Since it switched to the track in 1978, the Canadian Grand Prix has thrown up some great races. That first was probably the most popular, when Villeneuve won his maiden triumph under the adoring eyes of his countrymen, but his chase for the lead of the 1981 event, on a wet track and with his Ferrari's nose wing skewed skyward after a collision, still lingers in the memory. In 1982 there was tragedy on the old startline when Didier Pironi stalled his Ferrari at the start and was rammed by newcomer Riccardo Paletti, who died.

That race yielded a surprise victory to Nelson Piquet's turbocharged Brabham-BMW, and it was the Brazilian who took one of the most startling victories in the 1991 race, taking the lead on the last lap in his Benetton after Nigel Mansell, who had led easily, allowed his Renault V10's revs to drop too much as he negotiated the hairpin. To his chagrin his Williams was unable to pick up speed again, and rolled to a silent halt as the crowd watched in complete astonishment, and journalists began frantically backspacing their 'Mansell Walks It' stories.

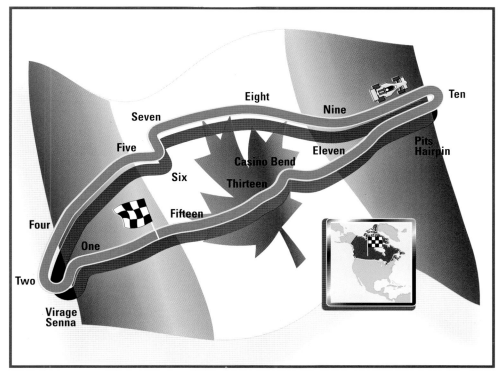

**CIRCUIT LENGTH:** 4.430 km (2.750 miles)
**LOCATION:** Ile Notre Dame, Montreal, Quebec H3C 1A0. Via University Street to Bonaventura Highway, first exit 'Parc des Iles', or undergound to Ile Sainte-Hélène station. Tel: 00 1 514 392 4731
**RACE DISTANCE:** 68 laps
**1995 POLE POSITION:** Schumacher 1 m 27.661 s
**1995 WINNER:** Alesi 1 h 44 m 54.171 s
**1995 FASTEST LAP:** Schumacher 1 m 29.174 s

# FRENCH GRAND PRIX

## Circuit de Nevers Magny-Cours, Nevers

TO THOSE WHO WERE UNFORTUNATE enough to go to the first French Grand Prix to be held at the Circuit de Nevers Magny-Cours, back in 1991, the place will always evoke memories not of the great duel between Mansell and Prost which an intransigent Andrea de Cesaris managed to ruin by refusing to be lapped, but of the sheer mayhem occasioned that week by the French truck drivers' strike. Seizing on the opportunity to further their cause, they made life hell for everyone.

Since then things have settled down and, as is the way with these situations in F1, the circuit has been accepted as the home of the French Grand Prix, the oldest Grand Prix on the calendar. Like most modern venues it is short of places to overtake, the layout combining a first-gear hairpin with several fourth/fifth-gear constant radius corners and a chicane, and doubling back on itself in a series of awkward curves. The biggest drawback, as far as the teams are concerned, is its billiard-table smoothness. This might sound odd given how much drivers tend to moan about bumps on other circuits, but therein lies the reason. Because there are so few other tracks devoid of the ripples and surface undulations that can make life hell when your backside is sitting only an inch above the deck and your car's suspension amounts only to the flexure of the suspension components themselves and the tyre sidewalls, Magny-Cours can be a difficult place to set a car up for. In Ligier's case the boot is on the other foot, because this is home base, where most of its testing is done. That's why the French cars often go so well in their home race, but struggle to reach the same level of operational efficiency elsewhere. A car that has been developed and honed on a smooth surface is not going to work as well on bumps.

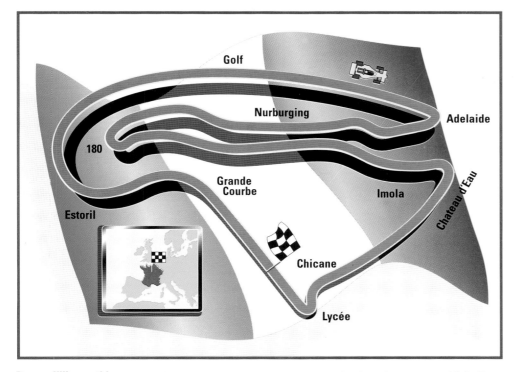

**CIRCUIT LENGTH:** 4.271 km (2.654 miles)

**LOCATION:** Circuit de Nevers Magny-Cours, Technopole, 58470. 250 km (155 miles) south of Paris, 80 km (50 miles) east of Bourges, 12 km (7.5 miles) south of Nevers on N7.

Tel: 33 8 621 8000

**RACE DISTANCE:** 72 laps

**1995 POLE POSITION:** Hill 1 m 17.225 s

**1995 WINNER:** Schumacher 1 h 38 m 28.429 s

**1995 FASTEST LAP:** Schumacher 1 m 20.218 s

**FRANCE**

**Damon Hill was this** *close to his first GP win in the 1993 race as he dogged team-mate Alain Prost.*

In 1992 Mansell repeated his triumph from the previous year in a Williams FW14B whose active suspension was perfectly suited to the track surface. Further back, the relationship between new boy Schumacher and reigning champion Senna was not enhanced when the German inadvertently assaulted the Brazilian in a contretemps on the first lap which earned him Senna's anger in a public dressing down prior to a restart. The Williams team repeated its 1–2 finish the following season as Alain Prost led Damon Hill across the line in a narrow victory that marked the great Frenchman's 49th of his record 51 victories. And afterwards the paddock gossip spoke of team orders that had decreed that Prost should be allowed to win on his home ground. Neither Williams nor Renault elucidated, though the latter said it was situation normal which meant they could both race one another until the last 10 laps. Hill had led from the start and looked likely to win his first-ever Grand Prix until a delay during his pit stop gave Prost the advantage, but thereafter the Briton sat right behind his team-mate and they finished less than half a second apart. It was the beginning of Hill's emergence as a World Championship contender. That was also the race where IndyCar champion Michael Andretti began to drive the way he had in North America, proving that you could pass at Magny-Cours by taking Alesi, of all people, in an aggressive lunge into the last corner. It would win him his first Championship point.

# BRITISH GRAND PRIX

## Silverstone, Northamptonshire

**CIRCUIT LENGTH:** 5.057 km (3.142 miles)

**LOCATION:** Silverstone, near Towcester, Northamptonshire NN12 8TN. 24 km (15 miles) south-west of Northampton, 48 km (30 miles) north-east of Oxford, 120 km (75 miles) north-west of London. M40 from London or M1 to junction 15a. Tel: 44 132 785 7271

**RACE DISTANCE:** 61 laps

**1995 POLE POSITION:** Hill 1 m 28.124 s

**1995 WINNER:** Herbert 1 h 34 m 35.093 s

**1995 FASTEST LAP:** Hill 1 m 29.752 s

**In 1995 Hill led** *at Silverstone from Alesi and Schumacher, but Herbert (fifth here) won.*

Copse · Maggotts · Chapel · Becketts · Hanger Straight · Priory · Stowe · Brooklands · Abbey · Vale · Woodcote · Bridge · Club · Luffield

**V**ERY FEW CIRCUITS HAVE INVESTED quite so heavily and consistently as Silverstone, the former wartime airfield in Northamptonshire, in keeping up with F1. One of the finest venues in the world, it is run by the British Racing Drivers' Club, whose managements over the years have always kept it in the vanguard since it won the exclusive contract to run the British Grand Prix after years of alternating with Brands Hatch. What now taxes drivers of Grand Prix cars every July is very different from the airfield whose runways were modified for racing in 1948 and where, on 13 May 1950, the World Championship was officially born. That day Giuseppe Farina steered his Alfa-Romeo to a victory over team-mates Luigi Fagioli and Reg Parnell that set him on the path to the Championship crown.

Silverstone has since worn many guises, but the underlying spirit that existed that day in 1950 still motivates those whose job it is to keep up with international competition, and to set the standards by which most other circuits are judged. It had only recently completed a major facelift for 1994 when the tragedies of Imola prompted further critical appraisal of circuit safety, and following a bizarre accident which befell Pedro Lamy during a test session, a further range of changes was initiated. Exiting Club corner on the slight uphill gradient towards Abbey curve, Lamy's Lotus had lost its rear wing and flown over debris fencing to land in the entrance to a pedestrian tunnel. As the unfortunate Portuguese driver recovered in hospital, the BRDC designed a new chicane between Club and Abbey, which would later draw high praise from Grand Prix Drivers' Association spokesman Martin Brundle. Other modifications were incorporated for the 1995 race, prompting cynics to question why, if Silverstone responded so rapidly and efficiently, circuits such as Estoril got away with situations that were so unsatisfactory. The questions went unanswered.

Today, drivers leave the grid and head for a tighter Copse corner, which now has greater run-off area. Maggotts is still a very fast flick before the third-gear Becketts right-hander gives way to a gentle left which leads on to the Hangar Straight, the fastest part of the course. Stowe corner is next; no longer a 90-degree right-hander taken almost flat by the aces, it folds back on itself and leads to the downhill run through The Vale towards a modified Club, itself no longer another steely 90-degree right-hander but now a slower 130-degree right. With less momentum cars then head for the new chicane and then on to the left-hand sweep that is Abbey, accelerating all the while under the bridge that gives its name to the next right-hander which brings them to the complex of left turns at Priory and Brooklands, and the double right at Luffield that starts them on the long right-hand curve through Woodcote. This is the famous corner through which Jody Scheckter spun his McLaren and caused a multi-car shunt in the 1973 race, which itself spelled the death knell for unfettered speed at the circuit.

Though the F1 paddock is such a fortress today that it keeps the super-informed British racegoers at bay, good photography is still possible from a number of spots around the course – and if you had the equipment you'd certainly have time to develop your shots while sitting in the traffic jam trying to leave on a Sunday night.

ENGLAND

# GERMAN GRAND PRIX

**Hockenheim**

**N**O MATTER WHAT CHANGES ARE made to it, and no matter how dramatic and exciting are the races it hosts, this is the circuit that will forever exist in infamy within the minds of true enthusiasts as the brutally fast but unimaginative track that killed the legendary Jim Clark on a cold and wet Sunday back in April 1968.

In those days Hockenheim was just a straightforward blast out of the stadium section on a curving track through tall pine trees until the road gradually bent back on itself and returned through more

pines until it popped back into daylight as it re-entered the stadium via a sharp right-hand bend. This led to a wide 180-degree hairpin with very slightly banked centre, before spitting you out on to a quick left/right dogleg and then the two final 90-degree right-handers that ended the lap. Then there was further respite along the pit straight until it was time to take your courage in your hands while keeping your right foot jammed to the floor for another tour of the dark pine forest.

For a long time now the outward leg has been interrupted by a tight chicane, while the backward loop, the Ostkurve, has another and a third is positioned halfway down the return leg. Anxious to jump on a bandwagon that belonged only

**CIRCUIT LENGTH:** 6.815 km (4.234 miles)
**LOCATION:** Hockenheimring, Postfach 1106, 68754 Hockenheim. 91 km (56 miles) south of Frankfurt on A5-E35, 113 km (70 miles) north-west of Stuttgart on A6-E50, 23 km (14 miles) south-west of Heidelberg. Tel: 49 6205 9500
**RACE DISTANCE:** 45 laps
**1995 POLE POSITION:** Hill 1 m 44.385 s
**1995 WINNER:** Schumacher 1 h 22 m 56.043 s
**1995 FASTEST LAP:** Schumacher 1 m 48.824 s

to Imola, Hockenheim followed several other circuits by naming the third chicane in honour of Ayrton Senna in 1994, at the same time taking the belated opportunity to name the first after Clark, a man it had largely ignored for the previous 25 years. There are those who believe that both men would have detested having such dreadful things as chicanes bearing their names. They consider this sacrilegous; chicanes are designed to slow cars, whereas Jimmy and Ayrton dedicated everything they had to going ever faster.

Hockenheim was first used to host the German Grand Prix in 1970, when Jochen Rindt's Lotus 72 won what appeared to be a close slipstreaming race from Jacky Ickx's Ferrari, though later it emerged that they had agreed to stage something of a show for the spectators. Rindt was so enamoured of the car that would kill him so soon afterwards that he claimed a monkey could have won in it that day.

More recently, Hockenheim brought heartbreak to Damon Hill four times in a row. In 1992 he failed to qualify his Brabham, while a year later he had his first Grand Prix victory in the bag after team-mate Prost had been given a questionable penalty, only to suffer a puncture within sight of success. In 1994 he spun away possible victory in a silly altercation with Ukyo Katayama, while in 1995 he was leading Schumacher on the latter's home ground, desperately anxious to make amends for his mistake which had taken them both out of the British Grand Prix a fortnight earlier, when he spun at the first corner going into his second lap. Perhaps 1996 will be kinder.

For all its banality, Hockenheim is worth a visit, if only to see the depth of adoration of the home fans for the World Champion. There's a nice little museum there, too, which motor-cyclists in particular should enjoy.

**Michael Schumacher** *was unbeatable in the 1995 event, winning his home Grand Prix for the first time and giving his obsessive fans (far left) the result they had come to see.*

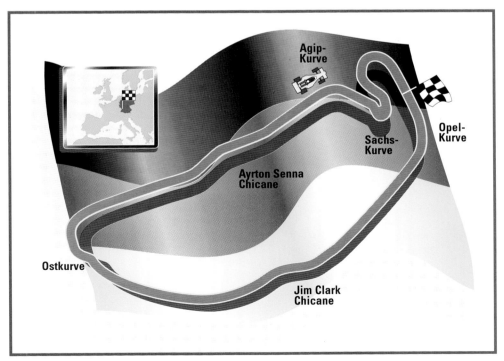

GERMANY

# HUNGARIAN GRAND PRIX

## Hungaroring

ONE OF THE MOST PLEASANT SURprises in recent F1 history has been the success of the Hungarian Grand Prix. The first race at the imaginatively named Hungaroring was held in 1986, when Budapest presented itself as a dark, grey place from which the export of such unlikely items as bread, toilet paper, Lego and brassières was expressly proscribed. Since then, as the Iron Curtain has been drawn back, the city has opened up like a blossoming flower, and now one's impression is not just of its sensational architecture, but its gaiety and colour. There is even a McDonald's, the saviour of many a racegoer and journalist alike!

The weather is usually blazing sunshine, which brings out Hungary's finest examples of both sexes, and the atmosphere is warm figuratively and literally in a paddock that, in August, is traditionally full of gossip about who will do what, and with whom, next season.

All of this is rather handy, because the circuit itself, though it possesses some quite nice features, has fallen prey to that great decree that overtaking shall be difficult, if not almost downright impossible. How else do you explain that in 1990 Thierry Boutsen, good racing driver though he undoubtedly was, was able to fend off Ayrton Senna for the entire race to beat the great Brazilian by a scant 0.288 s? In that respect the Hungaroring is not unlike Monaco, and it also shares another of the Principality's traits: after Monte Carlo it is the highest downforce circuit in the business. This, too, may explain why overtaking is so rare.

**Hungarians are** *enthusiastic fans of F1 (opposite). En route to a crucial victory in 1995, Hill (left) leads Coulthard and Schumacher out of the exit to the tricky first corner.*

one of the best sections, where a 90-degree right-hander leads back uphill, through an arc to the right, and thence to a sharper left. It was exiting the first right-hander that Mansell was able to pounce when Senna was momentarily held up behind Stefan Johansson's Onyx, and to go on to win the 1989 race for Ferrari; and the left-hander at the top of the hill where he had been lucky to survive an off-course slide the previous year.

Another 180-degree right leads drivers to the highest part of the circuit, which is still just visible from the main pit straight, and here is the chicane where Senna punted Alessandro Nannini out of possible victory in that 1990 race. The section that follows comprises the sort of left, right, left, right, right complex that provides no chance at passing unless the other driver makes an error, and then the final chicane precedes a sweep back downhill towards the sharp left-hander at the back of the pits. This is one of the better spectating points since this is where frustration often overrules common sense as drivers try for gaps that don't exist. After that a 180-degree right that mirrors the first turn takes drivers back on the main straight to complete the lap.

Budapest is a beautiful city to visit, and Hungaroring can be a fun place to sample a Grand Prix.

From the start/finish line it's the usual drag race to the first corner, a 180-degree right-hander that requires a lot more care that it might first seem, for the road drops away sharply close to the bend and the camber can pitch the unwary on to the outside line where it is easy to get elbowed into the dirt. A short straight leads to a gently descending left-hander, before the road drops steeply downhill to

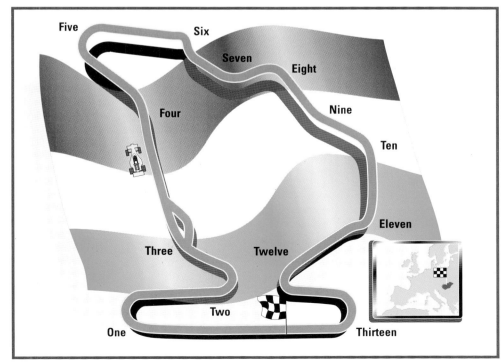

**CIRCUIT LENGTH:** 3.968 km (2.465 miles)
**LOCATION:** Hungaroring, 2146 Mogyorod – P.f: 10. 20 km (12 miles) north-east of Budapest on E71-M3 (sign of Miskolc, exit at 18 km/11 miles), 280 km (174 miles) east of Vienna. Tel: 36 28 33 00 40
**RACE DISTANCE:** 77 laps
**1995 POLE POSITION:** Hill 1 m 16.982 s
**1995 WINNER:** Hill 1 h 46 m 25.271 s
**1995 FASTEST LAP:** Hill 1 m 20.247 s

HUNGARY

# BELGIAN GRAND PRIX

## Spa-Francorchamps

SPA! THE NAME IS ETCHED IN THE minds of all true enthusiasts, for this is still one of the great circuits of the world despite the changes over the years. In the old days it was more than 12 km (7.5 miles) long, but in the early 1980s, when the Belgian Grand Prix flirted tragically with Zolder, Spa was updated over a more manageable 7-km (4-mile) layout.

Like the old Nurburgring, Spa presented a fearsome challenge, and still does, for this is a very quick track where the average speed is well over 215 kmh (134 mph) even though drivers negotiate a

or Alessandro Zanardi who lost his Lotus in qualifying there a year later, spun, hit the barriers very hard, and had swollen red eyes for weeks afterwards. Without question, Eau Rouge is a great test of mettle, commitment and accuracy. It is not the place for error, for here is where the great German talent Stefan Bellof was killed in the 1985 sportscar race during a frenetic duel with Spa expert Jacky Ickx. At the top of the hill, Eau Rouge gives way to the dogleg of Raidillon, before the long, long climb up Kemmel to the top of the hill at Les Combes, where Johnny Herbert snatched the lead last year from Jean Alesi. This is where the new circuit diverts from the old, as it turns sharp right, left, right at Les Combes and then spurts briefly to the 180-degree right-hander at Rivage, which then takes it back downhill to the sharp left at Malmedy, and then the very fast and very frightening double left-hander called Pouhon.

Pouhon leads to the sharp right/left at Fagnes, then the gentle 180-degree right at Stavelot which sets cars up for the very fast left sweep through Blanchimont and all the way down to the one spot on Spa's countenance, the ridiculous Bus Stop chicane, which slows cars prior to the short finishing straight.

Everybody should go to Spa. The *pommes frites* are wonderful with a little mayonnaise, and there is a great model shop in Francorchamps. And so what if it is always raining? Just put up your brolly, go to Eau Rouge, and watch high-wire artists working without a net.

**Slogans on the track** (above), *panoramic vistas – Spa-Francorchamps is the enthusiasts' delight. At the start in 1994 (left), Barrichello pips disqualified winner Schumacher to La Source.*

50-kmh (30-mph) hairpin and a fiddling little chicane during the course of the lap. The hairpin, La Source, is just beyond the point where poor Dick Seaman met his end in the 1939 race, and leads to the awesome downhill plunge to the corner that gives Spa-Francorchamps its great character. This is Eau Rouge, one of the Great Corners. It is approached at more than 270 kmh (168 mph), and at times the bravest have almost got through what follows without lifting.

What does follow is a curious corkscrew effect, for the road winds relatively gently to the left, but only momentarily. Then, just as the cars bottom out on their suspension bump stops, it flicks violently to the right while sweeping uphill like some tarmac rollercoaster, and almost as quickly, as cars crest its brow, it goes sharply to the left. This is not the sort of place where you want to emulate Perry McCarthy, whose Andrea Moda momentarily seized its steering rack under load in practice for the 1992 race;

**CIRCUIT LENGTH:** 6.974 km (4.334 miles)
**LOCATION:** Circuit de Spa-Francorchamps, Circuit House, Route du Circuit, 55, 4970 Francorchamps. 50 km (30 miles) south-west of Aachen, 50 km (30 miles) south-east of Liège. Via E40–A3. Tel: 32 87 275138
**RACE DISTANCE:** 44 laps
**1995 POLE POSITION:** Berger 1 m 54.392 s
**1995 WINNER:** Schumacher 1 h 36 m 47.875 s
**1995 FASTEST LAP:** Coulthard 1 m 53.412 s

# ITALIAN GRAND PRIX

## Monza

September 8

**The chicane blight** *at Monza frequently produces drama; in 1994 Eddie Irvine hit Johnny Herbert and created mayhem (above); Olivier Panis (inset) walks home to explain his 1995 gaffe.*

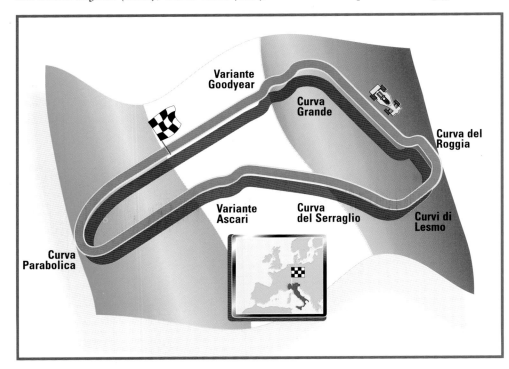

MONZA IS A SHRINE OF MOTOR sport that has kept the flame burning longer than most. The first Italian Grand Prix was held there as long ago as 1922, and though the old superfast banked circuit hasn't been used for a Grand Prix since 1961, or for sportscars since 1969, the ghosts still speak to you when you strain to climb to the very top of its crumbling 31 degrees. Eras have come

**CIRCUIT LENGTH:** 5.800 km (3.604 miles)
**LOCATION:** Autodromo Nazionale Monza, Parco Monza, 20052 Monza (Milan). 15 km (9 miles) north-east of Milan on SS36.
Tel: 00 39 39 24821
**RACE DISTANCE:** 53 laps
**1995 POLE POSITION:** Coulthard 1 m 24.462 s
**1995 WINNER:** Herbert 1 h 18 m 27.916 s
**1995 FASTEST LAP:** Berger 1 m 26.419 s

Variante Goodyear
Curva Grande
Curva del Roggia
Curva del Serraglio
Curvi di Lesmo
Variante Ascari
Curva Parabolica

and gone, and Monza has seen them all.

The circuit itself has changed remarkably little since its inception, though its speed has been limited by the deadly chicane blight. There is one, the Variante Goodyear, at the end of the long pit straight. Another, Curva della Roggia, before the infamously quick twin Lesmo curves. A third at Ascari, the corner leading on to the back straight where in 1955, only days after surviving a dunking in the harbour at Monaco, the great World Champion Alberto Ascari perished. He could not resist trying his hand in a new Ferrari sportscar, and in an accident never fully explained he left the road and was fatally injured.

For all its chicanery, Monza is a simple circuit, an uncomplicated speedbowl, from the hallowed Curva Grande, through the Lesmos, down beneath the overpass of the banked section, through Ascari and out on to the long back stretch that runs down to the two big right-handers that comprise the very fast Parabolica curve. It is inevitable over this span of decades that Monza would have seen tragedy besides Ascari's. One black day in

September 1933 the lovable racer-cum-opera singer Giuseppe Campari was killed in what was due to be his last race, and that same day Baconin Borzacchini also succumbed. Years later, the grim dashing of cup from lip would be repeated when Wolfgang von Trips was killed and fatally injured 14 spectators when his Ferrari collided with Jim Clark's Lotus approaching Parabolica. By cruel irony

Trips had only to secure a good result at Monza to become the first German to win the World Championship. Instead, the unhappy success fell to his team-mate, Phil Hill. Nine years on, Jochen Rindt's Lotus darted into the barriers at a similar point, killing him. Rindt did not live long enough to discover that he had already done enough to take the crown; he became the sport's only posthumous champion. And in 1978 Monza took the life of the much-loved Swede Ronnie Peterson.

But against the tragedies are stacked some glorious racing memories. It was at Monza in 1956 that Peter Collins helped Fangio to his penultimate title with an act of selfless heroism when he handed his own Lancia-Ferrari over to the maestro. 1957 saw the Vanwalls drub what owner Tony Vandervell called 'those bloody red cars' on their home ground, courtesy of Stirling Moss. In 1967 Jim Clark staged a breathtaking recovery to make up a lap and regain the lead, only to lose out in the last lap to fuel starvation and watch John Surtees beat Jack Brabham to the line by a hair. It was 1969 when four cars crossed the line less than two-tenths of a second apart, 1971 when it was five of them six-tenths apart and Peter Gethin won the fastest-ever Grand Prix at 241 kmh (150 mph).

As an enthusiast you owe yourself a trip – and take plenty of lire and treat yourself to the written word or memorabilia from Mario Acquati's inestimable bookshop right in the centre of this legendary track.

# PORTUGUESE GRAND PRIX

## Estoril, Cascais

ESTORIL IS ONE OF THE MOST popular venues with teams for winter testing. Just 32 km (20 miles) west of Lisbon and close enough to the edge of the Atlantic Ocean to pick up favourable weather, it is a like the Circuit di Catalunya near Barcelona: a mixture of fast and slow corners and elevation changes.

Like Barcelona, too, it has a long, fast pit straight, though the speed cars carry into the very quick double right-hander at the end prevents too many overtaking manoeuvres. These open sweepers lead to a short back chute before the track twists sharp right and climbs to an acute 180-degree left-hander. This in turn opens on to a fast downhill blast through a right-hand kink and on to the hairpin left at the bottom of the slope. Once again the circuit then begins climbing, this time to two 90-degree right-handers, before reaching the newest corner, the slow Corkscrew which is a very sharp left-hander that climbs steeply into a long right-hander. The Corkscrew has not been a lucky corner for Damon Hill. In 1994 he was inadvertently upturned there by Eddie Irvine; and in 1995 Michael Schumacher made the most of fresher tyres to dive ahead of his rival and cement another brick in the wall of what would become his second World Championship. After the right-hander exiting the Corkscrew, a

**CIRCUIT LENGTH:** 4.360 km (2.701 miles)
**LOCATION:** Estrada Nacional no. 9 – km 6, Alcabideche, 2765 Estoril. 32 km (20 miles) west of Lisbon on A5 direction Sintra/Autodromo (exit 9 or 10). 7 km (4 miles) north of Estoril. Tel: 351 1 469 1462/469 1412/469 1362
**RACE DISTANCE:** 71 laps
**1995 POLE POSITION:** Coulthard 1 m 20.537 s
**1995 WINNER:** Coulthard 1 h 41 m 52.145 s
**1995 FASTEST LAP:** Coulthard 1 m 23.220 s

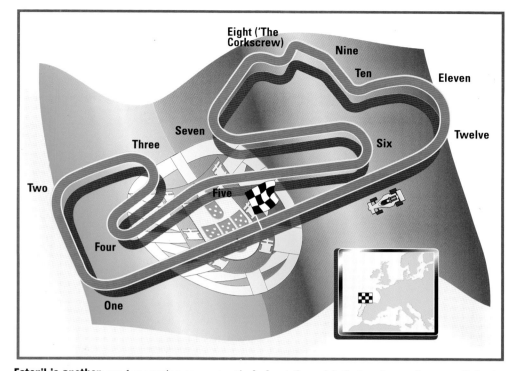

**Estoril is another** *good spectating venue, particularly at the quick first and second corners (below) or the Corkscrew (inset, with Alesi). In 1993 Hakkinen led from Senna to the first corner (left).*

90-degree left sets drivers up for the fast 180-degree right-hand sweeper which carries them back on to the pit straight.

The straight itself has seen its share of action over the years. In 1988 Ayrton Senna weaved violently at McLaren 'team-mate' Alain Prost at 290 kmh (180 mph), in a vain effort to frustrate the Frenchman's overtaking intentions, making team personnel on the pit wall pull themselves back in terror. Four years later, as Gerhard Berger pulled suddenly into the pit lane, the close-following Riccardo Patrese was caught unawares and was incredibly lucky to escape harm when his Williams-Renault became airborne. Only good fortune prevented it flipping over backwards. And in 1995 Ukyo Katayama's rolling shunt on the grid caused the race to be stopped and restarted. The pits, too, have played their part in Estoril's history. Who could forget Nigel Mansell losing a wheel in that botched Williams stop in 1991? Or Berger's alarming incident in 1993 when his Ferrari's active suspension malfunctioned over a bump and sent him shooting across the track right in the paths of J. J. Lehto and Derek Warwick?

And the first corner was the scene of a high-speed tangle between Mansell and Senna in 1989 when the latter's efforts to pass the former were rebuffed and the two collided. Mansell had earlier breached regulations by reversing in the pit lane and had ignored the black flag for some time, suggesting later that he had been unable to see it in the setting sun that shone in his eyes going past the pits. Had he obeyed the flag the incident with Senna would not have occurred, and the FIA banned him for a race for his trouble.

A year later Mansell cut across Ferrari team-mate Prost so sharply at the start, in a move that some still believe he cooked up the previous night with Senna, that the second-row McLarens were in the lead by the first corner. Mansell went on to win that race at a time when victory for Prost might just have given the Frenchman the World Championship.

# JAPANESE GRAND PRIX

**Suzuka**

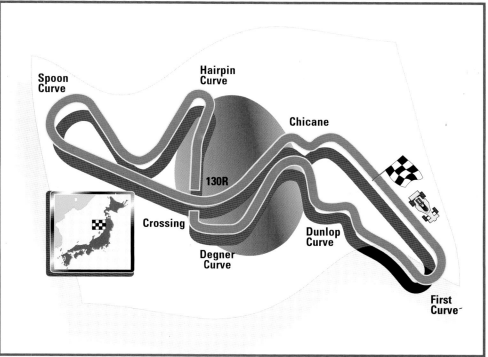

S TUDY A MAP OF SUZUKA, AND IT looks like something a schoolboy might fashion with his Scalextric set, complete with flyover section. But this is another great, challenging circuit. In places it is ferociously fast, and calls for maximum commitment, and like Spa's Eau Rouge, the oddly named 130R left-hander

**CIRCUIT LENGTH:** 5.864 km (3.640 miles)
**LOCATION:** Suzuka Circuit International Racing Course, 7992 Ino-cho, Suzuka-shi, Mie-ken, 510-02. 500 km (310 miles) west of Tokyo, 150 km (93 miles) east of Osaka, 70 km (44 miles) south-east of Nagoya. Tel: 81 593 781111/593 783405
**RACE DISTANCE:** 53 laps
**1995 POLE POSITION:** Schumacher 1 m 38.023 s
**1995 WINNER:** Schumacher 1 h 36 m 52.930 s
**1995 FASTEST LAP:** Schumacher 1 m 42.976 s

**With the amusement** *park as background (far left), Schumacher heads for a record-equalling ninth victory in his 1995 season, having dominated the Japanese GP from its start (left).*

demands nerves of titanium. The startline at Suzuka is on a slight downhill gradient, which proved Senna's saving grace in the 1988 race when he stalled at the start. Thanks to the slope he managed to stagger away, and then drove a superlative race on a slick surface to clinch his first World Championship. His subsequent two outings at the track owned by Honda, McLaren's former engine partner, were to be far more controversial.

The first corner is a wide 180-degree right-hander which immediately leads on to a series of S-curves before a very quick left-hand arc speeds cars to the Degner Curve, named after motor-cycle ace Ernst Degner. This is actually a pair of sharp right-handers close together, whose exit takes the cars beneath the flyover at 130R. Degner leads on to a fast straight and then a tight left-hand hairpin, and then cars regain their momentum in a long right-hand curve which ends in the tricky Spoon Curve, a long left-hander that has two apexes. This is where Hill and Coulthard went off in the 1995 race.

From Spoon it is a maximum speed blast all the way down the next straight and even through 130R, before hard braking for the chicane at which Senna and Prost tangled so controversially while contesting the lead of the 1989 race. Assuming drivers negotiate this baulky obstacle safely, they then accelerate through a right-hander to regain the pit straight. Perhaps because it has so often been the venue for races which have decided the outcome of the World Championship, Suzuka has seen more acrimony – certainly in recent years – than any other in World Championship history. After Senna and Prost finally had their long-expected coming together in 1989, the Brazilian's dramatic and brilliant recovery to victory was subsequently annulled by the sport's governors. The apoplectic Senna faced a ban the following season if he did not apologize for remarks he made in the heat of this argument with officialdom, and he was still smarting about the affair a year later when, in an act of chilling self-righteous indignation, he exacted his revenge on Prost. After an argument about the location of pole position, in which Senna made some quite fair comments but was still denied what he wanted, he vowed that if Prost beat him to the first corner he would not get through intact. Senna knew all too well that if the Ferrari once got ahead of him, its infinitely better handling would win the race and, in all likelihood, take Prost to another consecutive Championship.

Reliable observers say that when the Ferrari and the McLaren arrived at that first corner, in that order, the McLaren's engine note never wavered as Senna drove smack into the back of the red car and took both of them out of the race, in the most deliberately dangerous driving the sport has ever witnessed. The outcome of the title was thus settled in Senna's favour within seconds of the start of the race. Controversy apart, the sheer enthusiasm of the highly knowledgeable spectators helps to make Suzuka special.

# THE LURE OF RACING

**M**OST PARENTS WHOSE OFFSPRING HAS JUST VOICED the ambition to become a racing driver are usually put in mind of those words of wise advice: 'Don't put your daughter on the stage, Mrs Worthington.'

Between the extremes awaiting drivers of the talent, luck and success of double World Champion Michael Schumacher, thought to have signed a deal worth some $30m over two years with Ferrari, and the late Ayrton Senna, lies a minefield of euphoria, elation, anguish and disappointment.

The sheer risk to life and limb is one thing, something that had perhaps tended to get overlooked by most until events such as the tragedies at Imola in May 1994, or the career-ending injuries sustained by Martin Donnelly at Jerez in 1990, brought it back into painfully sharp focus. Beyond that,

though, can lie delusion, and for those who have tried and failed it can be like a living death. Like the theatrical profession, race driving has a cruel penchant for sucking people in and spitting them out into obscurity at will, long before they themselves are ever ready to quit. The circuits are lined with thousands of young hopefuls, some of whom got a long way towards the top before their careers levelled out and then withered. For every champion there are probably another 30 drivers who fail to make it. An unfulfilled life can be a tough thing to cope with.

On the following pages we present 12 of the very best Formula One drivers of the moment – Michael Schumacher, Damon Hill, Jean Alesi, Gerhard Berger, Mika Hakkinen, Johnny Herbert, David Coulthard, Jacques Villeneuve,

Heinz-Harald Frentzen, Martin Brundle, Eddie Irvine and Rubens Barrichello. In most cases it is more than obvious why they have been chosen as those who stand out; in others it is their potential and their position for 1996 that makes them worth assessing and monitoring as the season progresses. They are followed by 20 more, some with regular drives, others hopeful of securing them.

Life for racing drivers can be a great deal of fun and the rewards can indeed be bountiful, but consider for a moment the flipside that even those who have made it face. Consider the hours these men spend in gymnasiums honing themselves to withstand what amounts to a two-hour, 3g war with their car and the forces of nature; the constant pressure under which they operate, from team superiors, engineers, sponsors, media and fans (everyone wants a slice); and the frustrations that come with failing to realize one's aspirations. Then it becomes easier to understand why the acts of aggression come on the track, why the wars of words often follow disappointments, and why tears frequently flow when, having given everything you've got, you have come up short. In many ways motorsport is a microcosm of life; the pushy and the self-promoting tend to get on, while the shy and retiring are often pushed to the wall. It's sometimes sobering to remember that if these people weren't selfish, self-motivated achievers they wouldn't be there in the first place, and when they aren't saints you are often reminded forcibly that it takes a very rare breed to remain a nice guy yet still do what it takes to win.

Yet anyone who has ever held any kind of powered machine in a controlled slide, or who has successfully snatched a position on a racetrack, will understand the heady thrill of competing against oneself and others. And anybody who has felt the forces of nature doubled, who has been massaged by the vibration of a finely tuned mechanical animal that has remained within their control despite being pushed to its limit, will appreciate that there are some things in life that are infinitely preferable to sitting at home and watching others having fun. To these men this is life itself.

## Ferrari

# MICHAEL SCHUMACHER

| | |
|---|---|
| NATIONALITY: | German |
| BORN: | 3 January 1969, Hurth-Hermuhleim, Germany |
| LIVES: | Monte Carlo |
| MARRIED: | Yes, Corinna |
| CHILDREN: | No |
| PAST TEAMS: | Jordan (91); Benetton (91–95) |
| DÉBUT: | Belgian GP 1991, Jordan |
| RACES: | 69 |
| POLE POSITIONS: | 10 |
| WINS: | 19 |
| FASTEST LAPS: | 23 |
| WORLD CHAMPIONSHIPS: | Two, 1994, 1995 |
| HE SAYS: | 'I think Damon should shut up and drive faster.' |
| THEY SAY: | 'Michael is a cold character – we're never going to be friends.' – Hill |
| DON'T MENTION: | Adelaide 1994 |

**T**O HIS FANS HE IS THE NEW Messiah, the man who has taken the mantle of the late Ayrton Senna, and who would have beaten the Brazilian anyway if he had not been killed Imola. To his critics he is arrogant, prepared to stop at nothing to win. To his rivals, he is an uncompromising, aggressive driver who never backs down.

The moment that he stepped into an F1 car it was clear that Michael Schumacher was something special. He qualified a Jordan seventh for the 1991 Belgian GP, and though he burned the clutch out at the start, he never looked back. The controversy that has surrounded him ever since flared immediately after that race when Benetton poached him from the outraged Jordan team.

Much of that is water under the bridge, as are the allegations that he used traction control at some 1994 races, the FIA bans that kept him out of three races that year and deprived him of victory in another, and his ruthless disposal of Damon Hill in their great showdown clash in Adelaide. Now he is the first back-to-back World Champion since Prost in 1986, the man who won his first title sooner that Clark, Prost or Senna. By any standard the man is a phenomenon, one of those whirlwinds that engulfs a sport every so often and immediately assumes its right position.

**New car, new colours:** *Schumacher's switch to Ferrari has led to great expectations in Italy.*

## Williams

# DAMON HILL

**M**EASURED AGAINST MICHAEL Schumacher there is sometimes a tendency to see something of the plodder in Damon Hill. History has virtually reproduced the situation his father Graham faced when he was matched against the brilliance of Jimmy Clark. Yet both scenarios shortchange the Hills, both unusually determined characters.

It is a tribute to the manner in which Damon has developed his career that newspapers now identify his father to their readers through reference to Damon, rather than referring to Damon as 'son-of-Graham'. The family name might have opened doors at an early stage, but he has risen to his present eminence entirely by his own effort.

Just as Graham would have been the dominant driver of the mid-1960s without Clark, so Damon would have been the man to beat in 1994 and 1995 without

Schumacher, and it says much for his resilience that he came through a bruising 1994 with his determination and humour intact, despite team-mate Senna's death, and then being turfed out of title contention by Schumacher. Along the way he proved he could beat his rival, and that he deserved his seat with Williams.

The 1995 season was much less satisfactory when his overall lack of experience at times counted against him and his motivation was occasionally called into question, but, like Mansell, Hill fights best when he feels that the odds are stacked against him. Don't write off this deep thinker's chances of winning the World Championship this season.

**The son of a double** *champion, Damon Hill needed only one more win at the start of 1996 to equal his father's score.*

| | |
|---|---|
| **NATIONALITY:** | British |
| **BORN:** | 17 September 1960, London, England |
| **LIVES:** | Dublin |
| **MARRIED:** | Yes, Georgie |
| **CHILDREN:** | Oliver, Joshua and Tabitha |
| **PAST TEAM:** | Brabham (92) |
| **DÉBUT:** | British GP 1992, Brabham |
| **RACES:** | 51 |
| **POLE POSITIONS:** | 11 |
| **WINS:** | 13 |
| **FASTEST LAPS:** | 14 |
| **BEST CHAMPIONSHIPS:** | 2nd, 1994, 1995 |
| **HE SAYS:** | 'F1 today should not be a boxing match.' |
| **THEY SAY:** | 'Too nice a bloke for his own good.' |
| **DON'T MENTION:** | Alan Jones |

**Benetton**

# JEAN ALESI

| | |
|---|---|
| NATIONALITY: | French |
| BORN: | 11 June 1964, Avignon, France |
| LIVES: | Nyon, Switzerland |
| MARRIED: | Girlfriend Kumika |
| CHILDREN: | Charlocte |
| PAST TEAMS: | Tyrrell (89); Ferrar (91–95) |
| DÉBUT: | French GP, 1989, Tyrrell |
| RACES: | 102 |
| POLE POSITION: | 1 |
| WINS: | 1 |
| FASTEST LAPS: | 2 |
| BEST CHAMPIONSHIP: | 5th 1994, 1995 |
| HE SAYS: | 'If I have a problem with someone I prefer to have the explication, then the situation is closed.' |
| THEY SAY: | 'Still overdrives too much, too often.' |
| DON'T MENTION: | Martin Brundle |

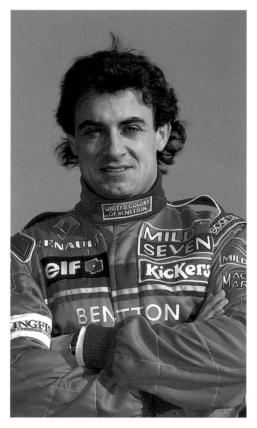

**A** CHAMPION OF ALL THOSE WHO FIND political correctness the tedium of the 1990s, Jean Alesi is a mercurial character who frequently acts before he thinks in matters where less emotional drivers might exercise caution and restraint. He is a racer whose heart is firmly attached to the sleeve of his overalls. When Alesi is happy, you know it. Equally, when something troubles him, there is no doubt about it.

One of the things that finally began to grate with Ferrari, to whom he has displayed commendable and unshakeable loyalty since joining the team in 1991, was his mood swings, from optimistic euphoria one moment to almost childlike frustration and tantrums of unalloyed rage the next when he felt the fates were against him.

At Monza in 1994, when he retired while leading, he slung his helmet at the wall of the garage and then stormed home to Avignon at maximum speed in his road car, with hapless brother José suffering silently alongside. It did not sit well with Ferrari.

In less charismatic drivers such behaviour would long have exhausted all patience, yet Alesi's dramatic style on the racetrack balances out his more juvenile excesses, some of which are the product of the frustrations born of uncompetitive equipment.

Few drivers are more popular with fans and media alike, and when he cried with joy after finally winning his first Grand Prix, at Canada on his 31st birthday, his were not the only damp eyes in the house.

**It is easy to forget** *the smooth style that Alesi exhibited in his early F1 years with Tyrrell, before frustration took over at Ferrari. This year, great things are expected of him at Benetton.*

**Benetton**

# GERHARD BERGER

'HE TAUGHT ME A LOT ABOUT OUR sport; I taught him to laugh.' Those words were Gerhard Berger's valediction to his friend, Ayrton Senna.

Those who have come to know the lanky Austrian well know that his sense of humour, at times somewhat macabre, has passed into Formula One legend. Who else could throw Senna's briefcase from a hovering helicopter, claim to have filled his room with snakes and frogs, or alter his passport photograph to resemble parts of the human anatomy that were not his face? Who else could douse a PR girl's computer with water, ruining months of work, and believe it a joke? Or deliberately provoke Senna, under the influence of a few unfamiliar Schnapps, to confront a mouthy Eddie Irvine at Suzuka in 1993?

If you can avoid being on the receiving end of Berger's jokes, it is not hard to see why he is so tremendously popular within the paddock. Then think back to the manner in which he escaped that fire at Imola in 1989, and was back racing within weeks, and to the depth and honesty of the emotions he explained to the press in the aftermath of the deaths of Ratzenberger and Senna, and you understand too that when he is in the cockpit a dedicated professional takes over. No man currently racing would make a more fitting World Champion than the man who makes female Japanese fans hyperventilate whenever they catch a glimpse of him.

| | |
|---|---|
| *NATIONALITY:* | Austrian |
| *BORN:* | 22 August 1959, Worgl, Austria |
| *LIVES:* | Monte Carlo |
| *MARRIED:* | Yes, Ana |
| *CHILDREN:* | Cristine and Sarah |
| *PAST TEAMS:* | ATS (84); Arrows (85); Benetton (86); Ferrari (87–89); McLaren (90–92); Ferrari (93–95) |
| *DÉBUT:* | Austrian GP, 1984, ATS |
| *RACES:* | 180 |
| *POLE POSITIONS:* | 11 |
| *WINS:* | 9 |
| *FASTEST LAPS:* | 18 |
| *BEST CHAMPIONSHIPS:* | 3rd 1988, Ferrari |
| *HE SAYS:* | 'If I was driving the Benetton Johnny Herbert had this year (1995), I would be doing what he was doing with it.' |
| *THEY SAY:* | 'As quick as Alesi, and smarter with it.' |
| *DON'T MENTION:* | Paul McKenna's wife |

**After a difficult start** *on his return to Benetton, driving the old B195, Berger quickly got to grips with the B196.*

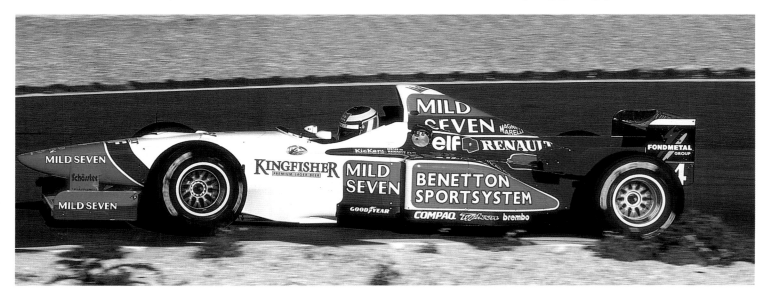

**McLaren**

# MIKA HAKKINEN

FROM THE MOMENT HE FIRST STEPPED into an uncompetitive Lotus in Phoenix, in March 1991, it was clear that Mika Hakkinen possessed the sort of talent to progress to the very top. Only the previous year the blond Finn had clinched the British F3 Championship after a tough fight with fellow countryman Mika Salo.

1993 was an odd year for the Finn. Leaving Lotus, he had joined McLaren but as team boss Ron Dennis already had Ayrton Senna and the American IndyCar champion Michael Andretti signed to race, Hakkinen had to content himself with testing duties until Andretti, who was finding F1 a tough nut to crack, finally returned to the United States.

By the time the Portuguese Grand Prix came around in September Hakkinen was desperate, having sat on the sidelines for so long, and actually outqualified Senna. Senna, meanwhile, was demotivated by the need to run a car that was no match for the Williams-Renaults, and barely as quick as the Benetton which used a superior specification Ford V8. Hakkinen's arrival was his wake-up call. The Finn never beat him again, but it was an

| | |
|---|---|
| NATIONALITY: | Finnish |
| BORN: | 28 September 1968, Helsinki, Finland |
| LIVES: | Monte Carlo |
| MARRIED: | No |
| CHILDREN: | No |
| PAST TEAM: | Lotus (91) |
| DÉBUT: | United States 1991, Lotus |
| RACES: | 63 |
| POLE POSITIONS: | 0 |
| WINS: | 0 |
| FASTEST LAPS: | 0 |
| BEST CHAMPIONSHIPS: | 4th 1994, McLaren |
| HE SAYS: | 'Senna never tested; I used to set the cars up for him.' |
| THEY SAY: | 'Not much happening upstairs at times, but a damn quick driver, in the Ronnie Peterson mould.' |
| DON'T MENTION: | Kissing Johnny Herbert |

**Approachable and cheerful,** *Hakkinen's future depends on how well he recovers from his Adelaide accident.*

indication that Hakkinen had all the speed he needed, and he spent 1994 and 1995 honing it while he learned about team leadership and racecraft. His serious accident in Adelaide last year cast a question over his future, but his speed in testing in February indicated that he has recovered fully and lost none of his fire.

# JOHNNY HERBERT

**B**ACK IN THE MIDDLE OF 1988 F1 teams were mentioning Johnny Herbert's name in much the same way that they would talk of Michael Schumacher in 1991 and 1992, for the Englishman was most definitely seen as the coming man of motorsport. British F3 champion in 1987, he won his first F3000 race and looked set to challenge for that Championship, while simultaneously putting in some dramatic testing performances for Benetton and Lotus in F1.

Then came a massive accident at the Brands Hatch F3000 race after a collision with the controversial Swiss driver Gregor Foitek. Herbert was lucky not to have a foot amputated, but recovered to score fourth place on his F1 debut for Benetton the following March in the Brazilian Grand Prix. After that politics forced his mentor Peter Collins from the team as Flavio Briatore took over, and Herbert's career fragmented as he was dropped.

When Collins bought Lotus he rescued Herbert from obscurity, but financial woes led to an acrimonious parting for Ligier, then Benetton again, late in 1994. In

**Herbert's return** *to Benetton in 1995 was a mixed success, but brought him his first two Grand Prix victories.*

1995 Herbert won two Grands Prix, but suffered badly as all the team's effort went into ensuring that Schumacher

| | |
|---|---|
| **NATIONALITY:** | British |
| **BORN:** | 25 June 1964, Romford, England |
| **LIVES:** | Great Alne, England |
| **MARRIED:** | Yes, Rebecca |
| **CHILDREN:** | Chloe and Amelia |
| **PAST TEAMS:** | Benetton (89); Tyrrell (89); Lotus (90); Lotus (91–94); Ligier (94); Benetton (94–95) |
| **DÉBUT:** | Brazilian GP 1989, Benetton |
| **RACES:** | 63 |
| **POLE POSITIONS:** | 0 |
| **WINS:** | 2 |
| **FASTEST LAPS:** | 0 |
| **BEST CHAMPIONSHIPS:** | 4th 1995, Benetton |
| **HE SAYS:** | 'I just wish Benetton had paid me the same attention it paid Michael.' |
| **THEY SAY:** | 'Jury still out on overall ability after controversial year at Benetton spent very much as Schumacher's number two.' |
| **DON'T MENTION:** | Career-threatening ankle injuries sustained in 1988 F3000 crash |

retained his World Championship, and he was denied the testing mileage that he sorely needed to set up a difficult and unforgiving car. Sauber could be his last serious F1 chance.

## McLaren

# DAVID COULTHARD

FROM THE MOMENT THAT HE GRADUATED from karting to Formula Ford racing cars, David Coulthard was impressively fast, hitting lap record speeds in his first trials. Assisted initially by rapid Scot David Leslie, he then came under the auspices of Jackie Stewart and his career progressed quickly through Formula Three to F3000. When Senna was killed, Williams snapped him up as the Brazilian's replacement, as Renault Sport entered into negotiations with Nigel Mansell.

Only an ignition problem stopped Coulthard finishing third in his first Grand Prix, and as he alternated with Mansell during 1994 he did sufficient to confirm his potential. At the end of the season Williams opted for the youngster's promise in preference

to Mansell's proven ability, and signed him to partner Damon Hill. Throughout 1995 he was fast – quick enough to set five pole positions and two fastest laps – but unlucky. Victories at Spa and Monza slipped away through mechanical unreliability, and it was not until Portugal that he finally made the breakthrough. But there were mistakes, too, such as spinning on the warm-up laps at Monza and Nurburgring, spinning and crashing in Suzuka, and the embarrassing collision with the pit wall while leading in Adelaide.

Coulthard is young enough and sufficiently polished to ride out such problems, and in the nurturing environment of McLaren is set to progress rapidly as a driver. Currently, everything will depend upon how quick he is compared with

**Urbane, articulate and** *polished, David Coulthard showed speed and flair with Williams in the second half of 1995.*

team-mate Mika Hakkinen. Scotland sees in him its greatest hope since Clark and Stewart.

| | |
|---|---|
| **NATIONALITY:** | Scottish |
| **BORN:** | 27 March 1971, Twynholm, Scotland |
| **LIVES:** | London and Monte Carlo |
| **MARRIED:** | Girlfriend, Andrea |
| **CHILDREN:** | No |
| **PAST TEAM:** | Williams (94–) |
| **DEBUT:** | Spanish GP 1994, Williams |
| **RACES:** | 25 |
| **POLE POSITIONS:** | 5 |
| **WINS:** | 1 |
| **FASTEST LAPS:** | 4 |
| **BEST CHAMPIONSHIPS:** | 3rd 1995, Williams |
| **HE SAYS:** | 'I've seen nothing to be frightened of at McLaren.' |
| **THEY SAY:** | 'Quick, pleasant and intelligent, but too smoothly packaged?' |
| **DON'T MENTION:** | Spinning on warm-up laps/ spinning in pit lanes |

# JACQUES VILLENEUVE

also a strong enough combination to win the overall CART PPG IndyCar title.

You'll find plenty prepared to say that he will find F1 a much tougher prospect, but Villeneuve immediately impressed with some quick times in testing, and exhibited a startling ability to learn fast and provide precise feedback. The manner in which he progresses will undoubtedly be a fascinating aspect of the 1996 season, not least because his style is so different to his father's. He certainly possesses the same free spirit; his dress sense has been described by his team as 'high grunge', and there have been doubts whether he owns a comb, but he is quick. And that is what counts.

**Even before the** *season began, Villeneuve had made a big impression on Williams.*

| | |
|---|---|
| **NATIONALITY:** | Canadian |
| **BORN:** | 9 April 1971, St-Jean-sur-Richelieu, Quebec |
| **LIVES:** | Monte Carlo |
| **MARRIED:** | No |
| **CHILDREN:** | No |
| **PAST TEAM:** | Williams (96) |
| **DÉBUT:** | Australian GP 1996, Williams |
| **RACES:** | 0 |
| **POLE POSITIONS:** | 0 |
| **WINS:** | 0 |
| **FASTEST LAPS:** | 0 |
| **CHAMPIONSHIPS:** | IndyCar 1995, Team Green |
| **HE SAYS:** | 'If I can win in IndyCars I don't see why I shouldn't win in F1.' |
| **THEY SAY:** | 'Frank Williams was bullied into signing him and is taking a massive gamble.' |
| **DON'T MENTION:** | How it feels to be the son of the late Gilles Villeneuve |

**G**ILLES VILLENEUVE WAS ONE OF THE greatest racing drivers of his day, but as any comparison between Graham and Damon Hill is unfair to both parties, so it is wiser not to offer any between Gilles and his son Jacques, who graduates to F1 as Hill's partner at Williams. Better, then, to view what the younger Villeneuve has achieved in his own right, for it makes impressive reading. He made a slowish start in Italian F3 racing, but when he moved to Japan he rapidly established race-winning pace, and his move to North America's Formula Atlantic revealed championship-winning ability with Team Green. They moved to IndyCar racing in 1994, and Villeneuve further underlined his potential with a string of competitive performances, perhaps the most significant of which was finishing a close second at Indianapolis on his first attempt at America's most glamorous race. Back in 1963 Jim Clark did the same.

In 1995 Villeneuve stayed with Green and, while triumphing at Indy, they were

## Sauber

# HEINZ-HARALD FRENTZEN

WITHIN THE SPORT FRENTZEN IS regarded as a great untapped talent. Williams, McLaren and Benetton were all interested in securing his services for 1996, yet he decided to remain loyal to Peter Sauber's small Swiss team for the final year of his contract. The two of them have been together for some time now, from the days when Mercedes-Benz

| | |
|---|---|
| NATIONALITY: | German |
| BORN: | 18 May 1967, Monchengladbach, Germany |
| LIVES: | Monte Carlo |
| MARRIED: | No |
| CHILDREN: | No |
| PAST TEAM: | Sauber (94–) |
| DÉBUT: | Brazilian GP 1991, Sauber |
| RACES: | 32 |
| POLE POSITIONS: | 0 |
| WINS: | 0 |
| FASTEST LAPS: | 0 |
| BEST CHAMPIONSHIPS: | 9th 1995, Sauber |
| HE SAYS: | 'I'm not afraid who I have as team-mate but my first choice is Patrick Head.' |
| THEY SAY: | 'Don't forget that in the Mercedes sports car team Frentzen was quicker than Schumacher.' |
| DON'T MENTION: | Losing girlfriend Corinna to Schumacher |

partnered Sauber to win the World Sportscar Championship. Back then, Frentzen's team-mates in Mercedes' Junior Team included Michael Schumacher and Karl Wendlinger, but where the latter stayed aboard in the hope that sportscars might lead them to F1 (as they did), Frentzen jumped ship to race in F3000 and came close to the plunge into obscurity.

With unusual candour he accepted his error of judgement, and when Sauber offered him a fresh chance for the 1994 season, the team's second in F1, he grabbed it and has never looked back. He was impressive straight away, and surprised the sceptics who had expected great speed allied to a penchant for falling off the road. The speed was there, certainly, but so was a new maturity. Small wonder that those who recalled how he had been quicker than Schumacher in their sportscar days began to seek his signature on a contract.

Whether this quiet German has made another error of judgement in staying with Sauber remains to be seen, but if the Ford-powered package works, expect him to be close to the front of races. Even if things don't go so well, he has already been tipped to join Williams next season, after turning down an initial offer at Monaco in 1994 after Senna's death.

**At Monaco in 1995** *Frentzen lifts a wheel in the Sauber. Already the big teams are talking to him about 1997.*

# MARTIN BRUNDLE

**Jordan**

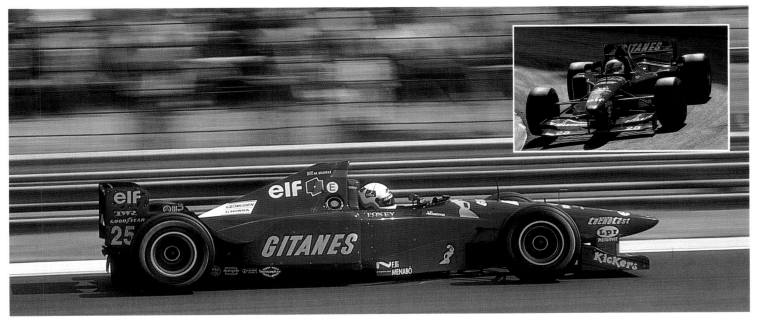

**Brundle's departure** *from Ligier (above in Hungary in 1995) brought parting from long-time mentor Tom Walkinshaw, but the opportunity at Jordan was too good to pass up.*

FEW DRIVERS CAN BOAST THE DEPTH of experience that has honed Martin Brundle into such a strong competitor. The Englishman's career took off in 1983 when he was matched against Ayrton Senna in the British F3 Championship. Despite nine consecutive defeats by the Brazilian, he vowed never to give up. On the tenth occasion he turned the tables, and thereafter their duel made this the best F3 series in history. Senna finally won through, but both graduated to F1 the following season, Senna with Toleman, Brundle with Tyrrell. Martin was fifth on his début and second only to Nelson Piquet in Detroit in only his eighth Grand Prix, though a row with the FIA later saw his points cancelled. Brundle came back from an ankle-breaking accident in the next race, in Dallas, but his career had lost some of its momentum. He raced for Zakspeed and Brabham after Tyrrell, but it was not until he joined Benetton for 1992 that he first got a break with a topline team. There, partnered with the emergent Schumacher, he

acquitted himself well after a difficult start, and was stunned to be dropped at the end of the year. If nothing else, he is a survivor, and after a season with Ligier he bounced into McLaren for 1994 after a nail-biting winter. Brundle's grittiness is just what Jordan needs in 1996.

| | |
|---|---|
| **NATIONALITY:** | British |
| **BORN:** | 1 June 1959, Kings Lynn, England |
| **LIVES:** | Kings Lynn |
| **MARRIED:** | Yes, Liz |
| **CHILDREN:** | Charlotte and Alexander |
| **PAST TEAMS:** | Tyrrell (84–86); Zakspeed (87); Brabham (89 and 91); Benetton (92); Ligier (93 and 95); McLaren (94); Jordan (96) |
| **DEBUT:** | Brazilian GP 1984, Tyrrell |
| **RACES:** | 142 |
| **POLE POSITIONS:** | 0 |
| **WINS:** | 0 |
| **FASTEST LAPS:** | 0 |
| **BEST CHAMPIONSHIP:** | 6th 1992, Benetton |
| **HE SAYS:** | 'I was always confident I could beat Senna in F3.' (He did) |
| **THEY SAY:** | 'A great number two but not fast enough to win.' |
| **DON'T MENTION:** | How long he's been in F1 |

## Ferrari

# EDDIE IRVINE

FEW PEOPLE IN THE F1 WORLD REALLY understand Eddie Irvine. It has been raised on a succession of intense, dedicated racing drivers who wear their hearts on their sleeves and would clearly donate body parts if it meant getting the right opportunity. Yet here is Irvine, insouciant, arrogant, honing his couldn't-care-less attitude – and partnering Michael Schumacher at Ferrari!

The Ulsterman has always appeared laid back; it was one of the things that held him back as he fought his way up the slopes of Formula Ford and F3. He made it as far as F3000 in Europe before the momentum sagged, as it often does, and then switched to the Japanese series. Before Irvine this had been regarded as something of a graveyard for Europeans who hadn't quite made it, but Eddie changed all that. He made plenty of money and won races, and used that as a springboard for two Jordan drives at the end of 1993, at Suzuka and Adelaide. In a sensational performance in the former he finished fifth on his début, and capped it all with that celebrated argument with Senna which resulted in the Brazilian punching him.

Since then he has shrugged off a three-race ban and matured nicely, reminding his friends of the late James Hunt. One fascinating aspect of 1996 will be how he tackles Schumacher.

**Controversial, yet** *compelling, Irvine reminds some observers of maverick World Champion James Hunt. Ferrari is his big chance to emulate the late star further by winning.*

| | |
|---|---|
| **NATIONALITY:** | British |
| **BORN:** | November 10 1965, Newtownards, N. Ireland |
| **LIVES:** | Dublin and Italy |
| **MARRIED:** | No |
| **CHILDREN:** | No |
| **PAST TEAMS:** | Jordan (93–), Ferrari (96) |
| **DÉBUT:** | Japanese GP 1993, Jordan |
| **RACES:** | 32 |
| **POLE POSITIONS:** | 0 |
| **WINS:** | 0 |
| **FASTEST LAPS:** | 0 |
| **BEST CHAMPIONSHIP:** | 12th 1995, Jordan |
| **HE SAYS:** | 'I told Senna I repassed him because he was driving too slowly.' |
| **THEY SAY:** | 'Too arrogant for his own good, and doesn't seem to care about anything.' |
| **DON'T MENTION:** | Punch-up with Senna after début race |

# RUBENS BARRICHELLO

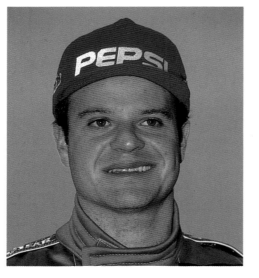

**W**ATCH RUBENS BARRICHELLO OUT on the track and you will be rewarded by a smooth display of driving. But watch him in a close fight with another competitor – be it Mark Blundell at Silverstone, or newcomer Jan Magnussen at Aida – and the results are slightly less impressive. This is something that has dogged him throughout his career, a problem he is desperate to address.

Until the arrival of Pedro Lamy, the Brazilian was the youngest driver in F1, and bounced into Jordan in 1993 on the back of victory in the 1991 British F3 Championship and a series of strong qualifying performances (usually marred by dreadful starts) in F3000. At Donington that year, in only his third Grand Prix, he was almost as sensational as fellow countryman and mentor Ayrton Senna, charging up to third place in the wet before running short of fuel. Since then, however, he has become pigeon-holed as a stylish driver who can't quite hack it in the sort of

on-track dogfights that a Senna or a Schumacher loves. There have been strong results, such as third in Brazil and second at Aida in 1994, or second in Canada last year, but he has yet to make the step up to the highest position on the podium. He needs the challenge new team-mate Martin Brundle presents.

**Smooth and stylish,** *Barrichello carries the mantle of Senna and the hopes of his Brazilian countrymen.*

| | |
|---|---|
| **NATIONALITY:** | Brazilian |
| **BORN:** | 23 May 1972, São Paulo, Brazil |
| **LIVES:** | São Paulo and Cambridge, England |
| **MARRIED:** | No |
| **CHILDREN:** | No |
| **PAST TEAMS:** | Jordan (93–) |
| **DÉBUT:** | South African GP 1993, Jordan |
| **RACES:** | 48 |
| **POLE POSITIONS:** | 1 |
| **WINS:** | 0 |
| **FASTEST LAPS:** | 0 |
| **BEST CHAMPIONSHIP:** | 6th 1994, Jordan |
| **HE SAYS:** | 'It helps having the support of my countrymen as the top Brazilian in F1 |
| **THEY SAY:** | 'A stylist like Gugelmin, but not a true racer.' |
| **DON'T MENTION:** | Why he doesn't overtake very often |

## Tyrrell

# MIKA SALO

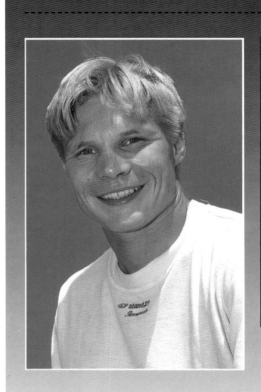

| | |
|---|---|
| NATIONALITY: | Finnish |
| BORN: | 30 November 1966, Helsinki, Finland |
| LIVES: | Helsinki and Chelsea, London |
| MARRIED: | Girlfriend Norika |
| CHILDREN: | No |
| PAST TEAMS: | Lotus (94); Tyrrell (95–) |
| DÉBUT: | Japanese GP 1994, Lotus |
| RACES: | 19 |
| THEY SAY: | Remember how competitive he was against Hakkinen during their F3 days in 1989. |

**Immediately quick in** *his first race, Salo was impressive throughout 1995 for Tyrrell*

**S**OME RACING DRIVERS MAKE IT obvious from the moment they first sit in an F1 car that this is where they belong, and Mika Salo is one of them.

Back in 1990 he and former boyhood friend Mika Hakkinen fought tooth-and-nail for the British F3 Championship, yet where eventual victor Hakkinen went on to join Lotus and establish his F1 career, Salo disappeared into the obscurity of Japanese racing. Then Peter Collins, who helped discover Nigel Mansell, offered him a drive in the final two 1994 races for Lotus. At Suzuka Salo jumped straight in at the deep end with a brilliant performance in a difficult car and in appalling weather conditions.

## Arrows

# JOS VERSTAPPEN

| | |
|---|---|
| NATIONALITY: | Dutch |
| BORN: | 4 March 1972, Montfort, The Netherlands |
| LIVES: | Montfort and London |
| MARRIED: | No |
| CHILDREN: | No |
| PAST TEAMS: | Benetton (94); Simtek (95) |
| DÉBUT: | Brazilian GP 1994, Benetton |
| RACES: | 15 |
| THEY SAY: | Super-quick but thrown in at the deep end as Schumacher's on-off partner in 1994. |

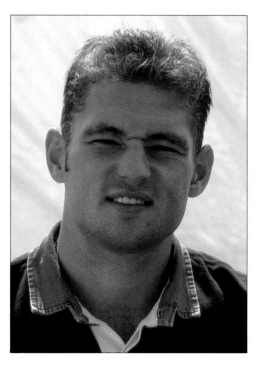

**Thrown in at the** *deep end with Benetton in 1994, Verstappen managed to swim.*

**A** DOMINANT VICTORY IN THE 1993 German F3 Championship led to a test for Arrows at Estoril, in which he proved very quick. Benetton boss Flavio Briatore then snatched him from beneath McLaren's nose, and when number two driver J.J. Lehto was injured in a testing accident he stepped in as Michael Schumacher's team-mate to make his début in the opening race of the year, the Brazilian GP. It was only his 50th car race.

He calmly shrugged off an accident with Eddie Irvine – and later on a horrifying pit lane fire at Hockenheim – to make a strong impression and went on to take third place in the Hungarian Grand Prix, but he missed most of 1995 when the Simtek team folded. A potential star of the future.

# OLIVIER PANIS

| | |
|---|---|
| **NATIONALITY:** | French |
| **BORN:** | 2 September 1966, Lyons, France |
| **LIVES:** | Grenoble, France |
| **MARRIED:** | Yes, Anne |
| **CHILDREN:** | Aurelien |
| **PAST TEAMS:** | Ligier (94–) |
| **DÉBUT:** | Brazilian GP 1994, Ligier |
| **RACES:** | 33 |
| **THEY SAY:** | Promising start in 1994, disappointing 1995 |

**Impressive in 1994,** *Panis had a tougher season in 1995 against Martin Brundle. Needs a good year to boost his confidence.*

APART FROM A PENCHANT FOR jumping starts (which led directly in 1995 to the governing body installing electronic detection sensors on every grid position), Olivier Panis made a strong impression on his F1 début in 1994. Driving for Ligier he finished 15 of his 16 races, and took a lucky but merited second place in Germany after the front runners met trouble.

His second season proved less promising and he was rarely able to match the pace of partner Martin Brundle. He typifies the F1 saying that you are generally only as good as your last race, and despite being a lucky second again in the 1995 Australian GP, he badly needs to revive a flagging reputation if his career is to progress beyond 1996.

# JAN MAGNUSSEN

JAN MAGNUSSEN'S STUNNING form in dominating the British F3 Championship in 1994 – he won 14 of his 16 races that year – caught the eye of all F1 teams and he soon became a part of McLaren's testing line-up to groom him for racing.

In 1995 he broke a leg in a scooter accident while contesting Germany's DTM saloon-car series for Mercedes, but bounced back to win his first race. Better still, on his F1 début standing in for Mika Hakkinen at the Pacific GP, he drove superbly to finish an unruffled 10th. He still hasn't got a regular racing berth in F1, but undoubtedly has a great future.

| | |
|---|---|
| **NATIONALITY:** | Danish |
| **BORN:** | 4 July 1973, Roskilde, Denmark |
| **LIVES:** | Silverstone, England |
| **MARRIED:** | No |
| **CHILDREN:** | No |
| **PAST TEAMS:** | McLaren (95) |
| **DÉBUT:** | Pacific GP 1995, McLaren |
| **RACES:** | 1 |
| **THEY SAY:** | Won more F3 races in a season than Senna; possible heir-apparent to the Brazilian star. |

**Magnussen:** *the next Senna?*

## Hopeful

# GIANNI MORBIDELLI

**M**ORBIDELLI HAS BEEN AROUND a long time without making the impression that his talent deserves. Third place in the 1995 Australian race owed everything to the misfortune of others, yet back in 1991, when he replaced Prost at Ferrari, he drove extremely well to take sixth place.

The Arrows team thought very highly of him in 1995, but he risks the same fate as similarly promising drivers such as Alessandro Zanardi, J.J. Lehto and Nicola Larini. Like many good midfield contenders, he needs to make the breakthrough with solid results if he is to move up.

Unfortunately, unless you get into the right team early enough in F1, this can be virtually impossible.

| | |
|---|---|
| **NATIONALITY:** | Italian |
| **BORN:** | 13 January 1968, Pesaro, Italy |
| **LIVES:** | Monte Carlo |
| **MARRIED:** | No |
| **CHILDREN:** | No |
| **PAST TEAMS:** | Dallara (90); Minardi (90–92); Ferrari (91); Arrows (94–) |
| **DÉBUT:** | Brazilian GP 1990, Dallara |
| **RACES:** | 60 |
| **THEY SAY:** | Far better than his patchy results suggest. |

**Trapped in the F1** *money vacuum, Morbidelli may have reached the end of the road.*

## Tyrrell

# UKYO KATAYAMA

**I**N 1994 KATAYAMA LAID CLAIM TO BE the most promising Japanese driver ever to sit in an F1 car, with a string of impressive qualifying performances for Tyrrell. Sadly, he rarely managed to convert them into decent race results, but the potential appeared to be there. It seemed all he needed was a little more self-control and a lot more luck.

In 1995 he suffered a setback when new team-mate Mika Salo consistently outqualified him, even on circuits Salo had never seen before, and usually outraced him. A number of accidents also eroded his relationship with the team and did tremendous damage to his self-esteem and usual confidence. More than most, he needs reliable results this year if he is to keep progressing.

| | |
|---|---|
| **NATIONALITY:** | Japanese |
| **BORN:** | 29 May 1963 Tokyo, Japan |
| **LIVES:** | Redhill, Surrey, UK and Monte Carlo |
| **MARRIED:** | Yes, Rumiko |
| **CHILDREN:** | Ryui and Risa |
| **PAST TEAMS:** | Venturi Larrousse (92) |
| **DÉBUT:** | South African GP 1992, Venturi Larrousse |
| **RACES:** | 62 |
| **THEY SAY:** | Best Japanese driver in F1 history but crashes too often |

**Destroyed in 1995** *by team-mate Mika Salo's speed, Japan's best-ever F1 driver is set to bounce back in 1996.*

# LUCA BADOER

**S**OMETHING OF AN ENIGMA IN F1, the quiet Badoer can be a difficult man to quantify.

In 1993 he often outqualified his highly experienced team-mate Michele Alboreto (a former winner for Tyrrell and Ferrari) in Scuderia Italia's uncompetitive Lola-Ferraris, yet he fudged possibilities at Benetton with poor timekeeping and testing performances for the team during the off-season.

Last year he had some good races for Minardi, although his reluctance to be lapped did not win him friends in the top teams, and he blotted his copybook by crashing a Ferrari during a public demonstration. Forti likes him, though, but unless he strikes it lucky he faces the same fate as countryman Morbidelli.

| | |
|---|---|
| **NATIONALITY:** | Italian |
| **BORN:** | 25 January 1971, Montebelluna, Italy |
| **LIVES:** | Montebelluna |
| **MARRIED:** | No |
| **CHILDREN:** | No |
| **PAST TEAMS:** | Scuderia Italia (93); Minardi (95) |
| **DÉBUT:** | South African GP 1993, Scuderia Italia |
| **RACES:** | 29 |
| **THEY SAY:** | Patchy career, hard to assess until he gets a more competitive car |

**Enigmatic and shy,** *the 25-year-old from Montebelluna has had an up and down career in F1, but was rescued by Forti.*

# PEDRO LAMY

**W**HEN HE CAME INTO F1 AS Johnny Herbert's partner at Lotus, Lamy never managed to capture his promising F3000 form. The 1994 Lotus was very difficult to drive, and he seemed cowed by it. In May he broke both legs very badly when the rear wing fell off during a test session at Silverstone, and it seemed his career had ended.

He returned in 1995 to race for Minardi, and immediately seemed better able to demonstrate his talent with stylish performances that eclipsed Badoer. But the jury is still out on this young driver who faced a daunting recovery so early in his career.

| | |
|---|---|
| **NATIONALITY:** | Portuguese |
| **BORN:** | 20 March 1972, Aldeia Galega, Portugal |
| **LIVES:** | Lisbon, Portugal |
| **MARRIED:** | No |
| **CHILDREN:** | No |
| **PAST TEAMS:** | Lotus (94); Minardi (95–) |
| **DÉBUT:** | Italian GP 1993, Lotus |
| **RACES:** | 16 |
| **THEY SAY:** | Lacklustre start with Lotus; looked more promising against Badoer at Minardi in 1995 |

**Fully recovered** *from his horrific 1994 shunt.*

# RICARDO ROSSET

| | |
|---|---|
| NATIONALITY: | Brazilian |
| BORN: | 27 July 1968, |
| | São Paulo, Brazil |
| LIVES: | Cambridge, England and |
| | São Paulo |
| MARRIED: | Girlfriend Michelle |
| CHILDREN: | No |
| PAST TEAMS: | – |
| DÉBUT: | – |
| RACES: | 0 |
| THEY SAY: | Quick; ran away with |
| | initial F3000 races in 1995 |
| | and looked a likely |
| | champion until overhauled |
| | by team-mate Sospiri. |

**A smart thinker** *in the Alain Prost mould,*
*Brazil's latest F1 graduate is learning fast.*

**L**IKE MAURICIO GUGELMIN WITH
Ayrton Senna in the old days, Ricardo
Rosset shares a house with fellow Brazilian
racer Rubens Barrichello, so he is well
poised for his graduation to the world of F1
with Arrows.

In 1995 he built on the F3 victory he
had taken at Snetterton for Fortec in
1994 by winning his first F3000 race, at
Silverstone. He won at Enna too, and
led the championship initially. A think-
ing driver in the Prost mould, who
spends hours pondering set-up, he is
also a successful businessman and
runs his own Track & Field clothing
company in Brazil.

His first taste of F1 came late in the
day, when he tested for Arrows at
Estoril a fortnight before Australia.

# ANDREA MONTERMINI

**W**HEN MONTERMINI'S SIMTEK
smashed into a concrete wall at the
Circuit di Catalunya, during free practice
for the Spanish Grand Prix in 1994, the
entire paddock was stilled, for here was
the man who had replaced the late Roland
Ratzenberger in the team after the
Austrian's fatal accident at Imola. For
moments it seemed that fate had cruelly
repeated itself, but, though knocked
unconscious, the little Italian had suffered
only ankle injuries. It was, however, an
inauspicious début.

He joined Pacific for the 1995 season,
and his blend of speed, brio and optimistic
humour impressed a team that was fight-
ing for its survival against mounting
financial odds. Like so many, he seeks the
right opportunity.

| | |
|---|---|
| NATIONALITY: | Italian |
| BORN: | 30 May 1964, |
| | Sassuolo, Italy |
| LIVES: | Rotegia, Italy |
| MARRIED: | No |
| CHILDREN: | No |
| PAST TEAMS: | Simtek (94); Pacific (95) |
| DÉBUT: | Brazilian GP 1995, |
| | Pacific |
| RACES: | 16 |
| THEY SAY: | Fast and impetuous, and |
| | better than his machinery |
| | has so far allowed |
| | him to look |

**Occasionally wild,** *but always enthusiastic, this*
*Italian charger has the charm and energy to*
*motivate teams.*

# VINCENZO SOSPIRI

**V**INCE, AS HE IS KNOWN IN THE PIT lane, has been pushing for an F1 opportunity for several seasons, since impressing in F3 and now, as the reigning F3000 champion following his best-ever season in 1995 with the Super Nova team.

Back in 1994 he tested for Simtek at Estoril, and immediately showed speed and commitment, but opted for a last effort to win the F3000 crown. This aim realized, he is now desperate to make his mark in F1, like his old F3000 team-mate, Damon Hill. The two remain sworn enemies after a number of clashes, but Hill has shown just what opportunities await those graduates with access to the right equipment.

Sadly for Sospiri, his hopes of a Ligier drive did not reach fruition.

| | |
|---|---|
| **NATIONALITY:** | Italian |
| **BORN:** | 9 October 1966, Forli, Italy |
| **LIVES:** | Forli |
| **MARRIED:** | No |
| **CHILDREN:** | No |
| **PAST TEAMS:** | Super Nova in F3000, champion in 1995 |
| **DEBUT:** | – |
| **RACES:** | 0 |
| **THEY SAY:** | Quick Italian overdue to graduate to F1. |

**Pushing hard for** *a drive in F1, the dogged Italian is knocking on the door of the upper echelon after his F3000 title win in 1995.*

# FRANK LAGORCE

**U**NTIL THE FINAL RACES OF THE 1994 F3000 Championship, Frank Lagorce looked sure to win the title, which has frequently proved a springboard to F1. Then a run of success by Jean-Christophe Boullion dashed his hopes at the eleventh hour.

He none the less raced F1 for the first time in Japan that year replacing Benetton-bound Johnny Herbert, but though he remained Ligier's nominated test driver for 1995, the cards failed to fall his way in terms of racing opportunities. There was talk of a drive for Ligier for 1996, but he was left hopeful of organizing something with one of the smaller teams.

| | |
|---|---|
| **NATIONALITY:** | French |
| **BORN:** | 1 September 1968, Paris, France |
| **LIVES:** | Paris |
| **MARRIED:** | No |
| **CHILDREN:** | No |
| **PAST TEAMS:** | Ligier (94) |
| **DEBUT:** | Japanese GP 1994, Ligier |
| **RACES:** | 2 |
| **THEY SAY:** | Another product of Elf's graduation system. |

**Almost a forgotten** *man despite an impressive list of past achievements, Lagorce could yet surprise.*

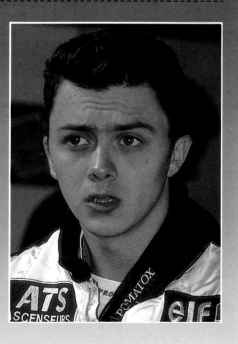

## Hopeful

# TARSO MARQUES

**C**APABLE OF BLINDING SPEED IN qualifying, this 20-year-old Brazilian also established for himself an unwanted reputation as a man prone to the odd driving error. At Pau in 1995, for example, he took pole position for the F3000 race, only to collide with DAMS team partner Guillaume Gomez at the first corner.

Balancing that, he drove well to take his first win at Estoril, and placed third in Barcelona. During the winter he impressed the Minardi team during tests, and clearly has a bright future at the top level.

He needs to calm himself down under pressure, but he is very young and has time on his side. He can afford to wait for the right chance.

**The best qualifier** *in F3000, but impetuous.*

| | |
|---|---|
| NATIONALITY: | Brazilian |
| BORN: | 17 February 1976, São Paulo, Brazil |
| LIVES: | São Paulo |
| MARRIED: | No |
| CHILDREN: | No |
| PAST TEAMS: | – |
| DÉBUT: | – |
| RACES: | 0 |
| THEY SAY: | Quick in F3000 Championship all through 1995, with plenty of potential. Showed well in winter tests with Minardi, and has bright future. |

## Williams tester

# JEAN-CHRISTOPHE BOULLION

**W**HEN JEAN-CHRISTOPHE 'JULES' Boullion went faster initially than regular drivers Damon Hill and David Coulthard during testing for Williams-Renault at the Circuit di Catalunya in Barcelona, it seemed that F1 had found itself a new star. The little Frenchman had just won the 1994 F3000 Championship, and looked for all the world like another emergent Prost.

Partly to assess Heinz-Harald Frentzen (in whom he was very interested), Frank Williams loaned Boullion to Sauber for most of 1995, but he proved a terrible disappointment, never seeming comfortable in the team, nor integrating himself. At a stroke his burgeoning reputation withered, and now his real F1 career may be over almost before it began.

| | |
|---|---|
| NATIONALITY: | French |
| BORN: | December 27 1969, St Brieuc, France |
| LIVES: | Paris, France and Oxford, England |
| MARRIED: | Yes, Alexandra |
| CHILDREN: | No |
| PAST TEAMS: | Sauber (95) |
| DÉBUT: | Monaco GP 1995, Sauber |
| RACES: | 11 |
| THEY SAY: | Set fantastic times as test driver for Williams in 1995, then disappointed greatly racing for Sauber |

**Fast testing a** *Williams, 'Dagger' Boullion disappointed racing a Sauber in 1995.*

# PEDRO DINIZ

**Ligier**

LAST YEAR NOBODY WAS EVER really able to prove or refute allegations made by drivers who had approached the new Forti team, to the effect that whoever joined would be contractually bound to play second fiddle to Pedro Diniz.

Such suggestions may explain why he was often quicker than his established partner Roberto Moreno. Or it may simply be that this son of a rich father (who had persuaded a number of large companies whose products were stocked in his massive chain of South American supermarkets to back his son's F1 plans) wasn't as bad as some liked to suggest.

With Ligier this year, we should finally discover the real truth about his F1 ability. And so will he.

| NATIONALITY: | Brazilian |
|---|---|
| BORN: | May 22 1970, São Paulo, Brazil |
| LIVES: | São Paulo and Monte Carlo |
| MARRIED: | No |
| CHILDREN: | No |
| PAST TEAMS: | Forti (95) |
| DÉBUT: | Brazilian GP 1995, Forti |
| RACES: | 17 |
| THEY SAY: | Son of a rich father, with more money than talent |

**Poor little rich** *kid? With a Ligier seat the Brazilian has his best chance yet for 1996.*

# TAKI INOUE

**Minardi**

1995 WAS DIFFICULT FOR THIS scion of a wealthy Japanese family, as he struggled to make his way in F1. At Monaco his car was struck — and inverted — by an errant course car while being towed from the circuit after practice; and in Hungary Inoue himself was struck and knocked down by another course car as he left his abandoned Arrows by the trackside.

Some would suggest the message was to give up F1, in which he proved a tardy contender in a car which Morbidelli showed was capable of running midfield. He typifies the 1990s pay driver, present by virtue of bank balance.

| NATIONALITY: | Japanese |
|---|---|
| BORN: | September 5 1963, Kobe, Japan |
| LIVES: | Tokyo, Japan and Monte Carlo |
| MARRIED: | No |
| CHILDREN: | No |
| PAST TEAMS: | Simtek (94) and Arrows (95) |
| DÉBUT: | Japanese GP 1994, Simtek |
| RACES: | 18 |
| THEY SAY: | Taki In The Way. Out of his depth in F1. |

**Inoue has a long** *way to go to prove himself in F1.*

## Ferrari tester

# NICOLA LARINI

QUITE WHY NICOLA LARINI IS NOT a fulltime F1 driver is a question best addressed to the management at Ferrari, for whom he has proved a perfect test and development pilote, and for whom he has stood in with notable result when its regular drivers have been indisposed.

Larini took the Ferrari role when his F1 career petered out after great initial promise with the small Italian Osella team. In 1994 he was second to Schumacher in the fated San Marino GP. When Ferrari signed Irvine as Schumacher's partner in 1996 it was too much for the Italian, who informed the management where they could deposit his testing role. Fortunately they have kissed and made up.

| | |
|---|---|
| NATIONALITY: | Italian |
| BORN: | 19 March 1964, Camaiore, Italy |
| LIVES: | Camaiore |
| MARRIED: | Yes, Barbara |
| CHILDREN: | Son Gabriele, daughter Nicoletta |
| PAST TEAMS: | Coloni (87); Osella (89); Ligier (90); Lambo (91); Ferrari (92 and 94) |
| DÉBUT: | Spanish GP 1987, Coloni |
| RACES: | 44 |
| THEY SAY: | Too talented to be out of F1; Ferrari wise to keep him |

**Underrated and quick,** *and friends again with Ferrari.*

## Ligier tester

# KELVIN BURT

IT IS A TRIBUTE TO THE ESTEEM IN which Kelvin Burt is held in some motor-racing circles that Eddie Irvine and Rubens Barrichello both found that they really needed to keep testing throughout 1994 when the Englishman was Jordan's nominated test driver. Each time he was scheduled to have a proper run in the car, the regular team drivers frustrated his chances. With an earlier test for Tyrrell, however, this former British F3 champion had already done sufficient to suggest a style reminiscent of the emergent Johnny Herbert, and in touring cars with Ford in 1995 he proved his versatility.

He will race Volvos and test Ligiers for Tom Walkinshaw in 1996, and great things are expected of him. He could be Britain's next big star.

| | |
|---|---|
| NATIONALITY: | British |
| BORN: | 7 September 1967, Tamworth, England |
| LIVES: | Lichfield, England |
| MARRIED: | No |
| CHILDREN: | No |
| PAST TEAMS: | – |
| DÉBUT: | – |
| RACES: | 0 |
| THEY SAY: | Just like Johnny Herbert in 1987 – great British talent on the brink if he can find the right opportunities |

**The next big British** *star, if only he gets the right breaks and a reasonable chance.*

# NORBERTO FONTANA

WHEN THE ARGENTINIAN NORberto Fontana was nominated as Sauber's tester at the start of the 1995 season, it aroused little interest from a media that was busy welcoming team driver Karl Wendlinger back to F1 after he had recovered from his Monaco accident in May 1994.

But on the track, Fontana took his opposition – which included Michael Schumacher's brother, Ralf – apart as he romped smoothly to the same German F3 title which had helped propel the elder Schumacher into the limelight.

Fontana's style is as unflustered as Prost's, yet possesses the aggression all quick drivers need. So far, his F1 tests have been limited, but he is very much a man to keep an eye on.

| | |
|---|---|
| **NATIONALITY:** | Argentinian |
| **BORN:** | 20 January 1975, Arreates, Argentina |
| **LIVES:** | Altnacht, Switzerland |
| **MARRIED:** | No |
| **CHILDREN:** | No |
| **PAST TEAMS:** | – |
| **DÉBUT:** | – |
| **RACES:** | 0 |
| **THEY SAY:** | Sauber test driver who showed tremendous speed and style in the German F3 Championship in 1995 |

**Quicker than Ralf** *Schumacher in German F3, but too short on F1 mileage for his own good.*

# KENNY BRACK

KENNY BRACK HAS BEEN HIGHLY rated by observers of the F3000 Championship for the past two seasons, and ended 1995 with a runaway victory in the last round at Magny-Cours. Overall, he finished third in the series in his Madgwick International Reynard.

Brack is an intelligent and articulate competitor who has good connections back home in Sweden. He is set for a very competitive season racing in F3000 for champion team Super Nova, and undertaking a 'driver development' test programme with the Ligier F1 team, after having protracted talks during the winter months with McLaren and Benetton as well.

| | |
|---|---|
| **NATIONALITY:** | Swedish |
| **BORN:** | 21 March 1966, Arvija, Sweden |
| **LIVES:** | Karlstadt, Sweden |
| **MARRIED:** | No |
| **CHILDREN:** | No |
| **PAST TEAMS:** | – |
| **DÉBUT:** | – |
| **RACES:** | 0 |
| **THEY SAY:** | Likeable, laid-back Swede in the mould of the late Ronnie Peterson. Showed well in F3000 and won final race of 1996. |

**Laid back, but** *very quick and determined.*

# HALL OF FAME

*One of the fastest ways to start an argument between motorsport aficionados is to attempt to list drivers in an all-time greatest order. It simply isn't possible. It isn't even feasible, truth be told, for how can one compare the era in which Fangio raced, for example, with Schumacher's? Back in the 1950s expectations of sportsmen were very different from what they are today. Then any media interest was centred primarily on the cars – journalists were far more intrigued by the thread size of bolts than by the situation between Fangio and his women.*

**Opposite** *The art of the master – Juan Manuel Fangio demonstrates what makes great drivers during the 1957 French Grand Prix at Rouen.*

**N**owadays there are those who feel they have fallen down on the job if they cannot ascertain how many spoonfuls of muesli Damon Hill ate prior to free practice on a Saturday morning. The pendulum has swung almost too far in the opposite direction, with intrusive probing into all aspects of a driver's character and behaviour and little interest in the technology of the sport.

Before sponsorship became essential and money began to gear the sport, some of the pressure on drivers was lower. In turn there was therefore less need for the sort of questionable driving tactics to pass a rival or keep him behind that we see all too often today. There was another more practical reason, too, as the great American Dan Gurney once remarked. 'If people pulled stunts like that they tended to sort themselves out in a hurry. You just hoped they didn't take you with them when they crashed!' Back then, in the days of tubular steel spaceframes and nascent sheet-aluminium cigar-tube monocoque chassis, drivers could not

have the same faith in their survival prospects if they left the road as today's carbon-fibre armoured knights, and bullying tactics were the exclusive reserve of the real mavericks.

Besides, which, what really defines a great driver?

None of the rules are set in stone. Even success is not necessarily a requisite if you look at the case of a star such as Gilles Villeneuve. It is a complex amalgam of so many factors: speed, talent, persistence, courage, success, charisma, humility, felicity . . . and a hundred more. Yet somewhere in it all lies an indefinable spark that makes a man special, that bestows upon him the gift of being able to do things on a certain day or days that no other could at that time achieve. On the following pages are 12 drivers from the Hall of Fame. It is, of course, a personal choice, for what else can these things be? And it is not necessarily definitive. Like taste in wine, cars, music or religion, to stick with the safer ground, choice of one's great drivers is something upon which only the individual concerned can truly agree.

# JIM CLARK
## A GENTLE GIANT

TO MANY, JIM CLARK REMAINS THE greatest racing driver in history. He won 25 of his 72 Grands Prix, and his victory in the 1965 Indianapolis 500 crushed the American racing psyche. He had a towering ability to get the maximum out of any car he drove, without appearing to be trying hard. Motor racing found in this gentle Scottish farmer a World Champion of great humility. Clark raced in an era when chivalry was still an intrinsic part of the game, and he never resorted to underhand tactics.

Races surrendered to his magnetic genius. He drove exclusively in Formula One for the innovative Colin Chapman, who more often than not produced the fastest cars. Clark certainly benefited from the first pukka monocoque F1 car, the Lotus 25, in 1962, and again from the power of the Ford DFV in 1967. Yet Chapman's wares were frequently fragile. Clark lost both the 1962 and 1964 Championships in the final races, through mechanical frailty, and had his Lotus 49 been more reliable in 1967 he would have triumphed then, too. The best index was how he performed in adversity, such as at Zandvoort in 1966.

Clark loved retiring to the tranquillity of the family farm in Duns, just over the border in Scotland, though in later years he became more cosmopolitan, less reserved and more relaxed in the international spotlight, more rounded in all respects.

He died following sudden tyre failure in a Formula Two race at Hockenheim on 7 April 1968, when his Lotus slid into a tree at high speed. He had no chance. His close rival Chris Amon spoke for a shattered community when he said: 'If this can happen to Jimmy, what chance do the rest of us have?'

**The gentle farmer** *out of the cockpit, Jim Clark became a tiger when he took the wheel.*

# AYRTON SENNA

## CHAMPION BY RIGHT

**M**ONUMENTAL GENIUS, FRIGHTENing commitment, and a willingness to go right to the very edge forged Ayrton Senna into one of the greatest drivers, and his record for 65 pole positions still stands almost two years after his death in the San Marino Grand Prix at Imola on 1 May 1994.

As with Jim Clark, the racing world had to adjust to the sudden loss of this mercurial man, but though Michael Schumacher has risen to don his mantle, just as Jackie Stewart did Clark's, the Brazilian star's passing has yet to fall into its full perspective. Only Alain Prost exhibited the same level of fanatical interest in the inner workings of his machinery, and Senna's ability to relate to his engineers precise technical feed-back not just from individual laps in different races on different circuits but – even more incredibly – in different years, has long passed into legend. That, and his innate speed and the willingness to push to the point where, at times, even he admitted that he felt as if he was having out-of-body experiences as a warning to ease back, made Senna almost irresistible.

Sadly, his tactics frequently bordered on the reckless, sometimes worse than that. As his team-mate at McLaren in 1988 Prost discovered that winning meant everything to Senna when he was almost forced into the pit wall at Estoril at more than 290 kmh (180 mph). In Japan in 1990 Senna's frustration at losing the title to Prost the previous year finally bubbled over as he deliberately rammed him out of the Japanese Grand Prix, and thereby recovered the crown he regarded as a birthright.

Ruthless and frequently misunderstood, Senna often did his best to hide a softer, highly emotional and compassionate side behind a self-constructed shell of aloof aggression. Yet this was the man who cried for Roland Ratzenberger and who, on the day of his own death, planned in victory to wave an Austrian flag as a tribute to his fallen contemporary.

*"I am not designed to finish second, I am designed to win"*

**No driver in history** *brought such a combination of raw speed, car control, cerebral intensity and pure ruthlessness to his driving as Ayrton Senna.*

# STIRLING MOSS
## THE UNCROWNED KING

THERE IS NO DOUBT THAT STIRLING Crauford Moss was the greatest driver never to win the World Championship. Where Fangio excelled in Grand Prix races, Moss was a brilliantly versatile all-rounder who could perform as well in gruelling sportscar events such as Le Mans, the Targa Florio or the Tourist Trophy as he did in Formula One. His dramatic victory for Mercedes-Benz in the 1955 Mille Miglia endurance race across Italy owed much to detailed route planning, but his innate ability was the predominant factor.

For Moss the manner in which the battle was fought was as important as the outcome, and this sporting attitude cost him the 1958 World Championship when he stood up for his main rival, Mike Hawthorn, who faced a penalty in Portugal that would, in retrospect, have denied him the points he needed to beat Moss. Stirling never for one moment entertained any thought of gaining an advantage in such a way, and stepped forward to defend Hawthorn, who subsequently went on to beat him by a mere point to become the first British World Champion.

Moss's active career in topline competition ended when his Lotus left the road at Goodwood at Easter, 1962, and he received serious head injuries. That left a twofold postscript to a fabulous career. What might he have achieved had he not stuck so religiously to driving British cars, or if he had accepted more offers of full factory drives instead of sticking with Rob Walker's private enterprise? And what might the future have held had he not felt obliged to rush his recovery, and been discouraged when his initial trials made him doubt that the old flair was still intact?

**Stirling Moss:** *the greatest uncrowned king in racing history.*

# JUAN MANUEL FANGIO
## ARGENTINA'S ICON

**P**ROST, SENNA, MANSELL, STEWART, Clark and Lauda all went on to win more than his 24 Grands Prix, but only Prost has ever come close to Juan Manuel Fangio's record of five World Championships, and the Argentinian, who died in July 1995, is still championed by many supporters around the world as the best racing driver there has been. In his lifetime he was revered around the globe as the epitome of the sporting champion, a short, bandy-legged character with a high-pitched voice and penetrating clear blue eyes. An icon who spoke no English, yet whose startling charisma was its own language.

He was a veteran of stamina-building cross-country marathons in his homeland, and from 1950, when the World Championship was officially inaugurated, until his abrupt retirement in the middle of 1958, he was the man to beat. Cool, unruffled and possessed of tigerish strength and endurance, he drove only just as fast as he needed to win, though as he revealed on days such as that at the legendary Nurburgring in 1957, he could take on and beat the world's best even though he was then well into his forties. In that race he deliberately started with a low fuel load and built a healthy lead, only to lose double that advantage in a disastrous pit stop. Undaunted, he returned to battle to challenge and conquer the young English lions Mike Hawthorn and Peter Collins in their Ferraris, to win the greatest of all his triumphs. Even Fangio admitted he had never driven so hard for so long.

*"During a race, I thought all the time that I was the best"*

A quiet, self-effacing character out of the cockpit, Fangio was a ruthless competitor within it, and had the killer instinct of the natural winner. And he could coax and cajole his machinery into giving a better performance, or into surviving long enough to finish. While he raced he was, like Clark, Senna and Moss, the yardstick by which others were judged, and judged themselves.

**A gentleman to the end,** *Fangio never did reveal whether he 'allowed' Mercedes partner Stirling Moss to beat him to the line in the British Grand Prix at Aintree in 1955.*

# ALBERTO ASCARI
## SLAVE TO SUPERSTITION

**N**OT UNTIL DAMON HILL CAME ON the scene did a second-generation racing driver manage to emulate a parent's feats quite as ably as did Alberto Ascari, whose father Antonio had been a star for the Alfa-Romeo Grand Prix team until his death in the French GP at Montlhery in 1925.

The younger Ascari did not have the look of a racing driver, his slightly rotund build earning him the nickname 'Ciccio' or 'Chubby'. Nor did he exhibit the traditional Latin trait of emotional excitability. Instead he was as cool a thinker as Prost, with the same extra edge of speed that makes a champion, and the calm unflappability that made any race he led a foregone conclusion. He was never happier than when he was out in front, breaking the opposition and leaving it to struggle. He was the only man truly capable of taking a fight to the legendary Fangio and coming out on top. If he had a failing, it was his intense obsession with superstition, to which he was a complete slave.

Alfa-Romeo was initially dominant with its supercharged cars when the World Championship began in 1950, but in 1952 and 1953, when the formula had changed, Ascari was in a class of his own driving for Enzo Ferrari's team. From mid-year to mid-year he performed the unrepeated feat of winning every race.

It was said that where Fangio would just miss a straw bale by the same margin every lap, Ascari would consistently clip it, living right on the edge. In 1955 he crashed into the harbour during the Monaco GP. A week later, unable to resist the lure of testing a Ferrari at Monza, he crashed on the corner now named in his honour. The death of Italy's greatest post-war driver has never been fully explained.

**Alberto Ascari** *was the only man of his era with the ability to take on Fangio regularly.*

# GILLES VILLENEUVE
## *ON THE EDGE OF RISK*

NO DRIVER IN THE MODERN ERA OF wings, ground effect, slick tyres and rock-hard suspensions has ever quite managed to capture the spirit and romance of motor racing the way that Gilles Villeneuve did. The record books attribute him six victories, yet such bald statistics ill serve his brilliance, and tell us nothing of his fierce (some said misplaced) loyalty to Ferrari, nor the code of honour by which he raced. At Monza in 1979 he refused to succumb to temptation to sneak past team-mate Jody Scheckter against team orders, in an effort to prolong his own World Championship aspirations, and that day Jody duly clinched his crown. Gilles applauded him warmly, confident that his own day would come.

*"The championship means little to me; Moss didn't win it"*

In a car as aerodynamically excellent as the Williams driven by arch-rival Alan Jones, Villeneuve would have been uncatchable; instead he chose to struggle with technically outdated Ferraris and was always spectacular as he compensated energetically for their shortcomings. Despite them, he would overtake where others said overtaking was impossible. When a car spun in a cloud of rubber smoke, lost a wheel, yet still tried to continue, it was invariably Gilles at the helm. He was the only one who could do things that conventional wisdom said could not be done.

His chivalry at Monza was stark contrast to the manner in which he felt team-mate Didier Pironi cheated him out of victory in the 1982 San Marino GP, by ignoring team orders. Feeling duped and betrayed, Villeneuve never again spoke to Pironi. Less than two weeks after Imola, he crashed to his death trying to beat Pironi's time in qualifying for the Belgian GP at Zolder. Some said it was the inevitable end, but for those to whom honour and love of racing were cornerstones, and who revered straight-talking racers who never gave up nor ever gave less than their best, a light went out in the sport.

**Gilles Villeneuve** *wove a tapestry of speed, drama and romance that racing had not seen since the great Tazio Nuvolari in the 1930s.*

# ALAIN PROST
## THE PROFESSOR

**I**T IS IRONIC THAT THE LATTER PART OF his career was sullied by his ongoing psychological battle with Ayrton Senna, for Alain Prost's achievements – a record 51 Grands Prix victories and four World Championships – deserve better than to be overshadowed by politics and acrimony. It is easy to see the little Frenchman with the shaggy hair and the boxer's nose as the man whom Senna deposed as king, and much of the comment that subsequently questioned his motivation was not only unjustified, but overlooked what he had achieved in the early years.

One had been at his peak for much longer than is usual, and the other was just approaching his. The key is that they were not at comparable stages of their careers. Look back a few years to 1984 and 1986, and you can see Prost playing Senna to Niki Lauda, himself once the pacemaker who played the role Prost would come to adopt – the role that Senna did not live long enough to have to consider in the fight with Michael Schumacher. To all things there is a season.

In his first year, with McLaren in 1980, Prost was outstanding despite poor machinery. With Renault between 1981 and 1983 he won nine races and established himself as a star. He lost the 1983 title through mechanical unreliability, and the 1984 Championship by a mere half point to the canny Lauda. In the ensuing years some of his early pace gave way to canniness of his own, and nobody could judge a race so beautifully as the Professor. He started the 1990 Mexican Grand Prix only 13th on the grid, paced himself cleverly in the early running, and won. It typified his ability to read a race. In the fuel economy era of the mid-1980s, he was peerless.

In truth, he and Senna were too alike for their own good. Take away one, and the other would have set records that might never have been challenged.

> *"It is a game, to be played to the full, to be enjoyed, with honour"*

**A very quick** *driver with the mental capacity to slow things down and the restraint to pace himself and read a race, Alain Prost equalled Senna in all but ruthlessness.*

# JACKIE STEWART
## *CAPPED CRUSADER*

**O**NE OF THE QUESTIONS GUARANTEED to keep motor racing *aficionados* arguing well into the night is just how Jim Clark and Jackie Stewart would have compared at their respective peaks. When Stewart came into Formula One in 1965 Clark was at the very height of his powers, yet frequently he was the only man ahead of the former Olympic standard clay-pigeon shooter from Dumbarton, who made a quite remarkable début.

Clark died before Stewart found himself a car capable of challenging for the World Championship, though their battles in the winter Tasman series in Australia and New Zealand in 1966 and 1967 had thrown up further interesting discussion fodder. Emerging from Clark's shadow, Stewart assumed the older Scot's role as yardstick, while also establishing his own unique image of long hair, Beatle cap and Rolex watch. He parlayed his speed and the ability to interpret a car's behaviour into a record 27 wins before retirement beckoned in 1973. By then he had also won three World Championships, and was one of the few to walk away from the driving side of the sport at the top.

His very style belied his raw speed. Where his closest rival, Jochen Rindt, was aggressive and flamboyant, Stewart achieved similar result with Clark-like smoothness and persistence, and the acumen for which his race is famed. It was easy to believe that his success came from being in the right team – Tyrrell – at the right time, and to overlook just how quick he could be, which was as quick as the best of them.

More than any other racer, Jackie Stewart revolutionized safety standards with a remorseless crusade for circuit and car improvements, and was among the first to pioneer use of safety-belts and full-face helmets. Short-term unpopularity with circuit owners has long since been superseded by an enduring affection for the spring-heeled little Scot who today prepares to enter his own Grand Prix team in the sport in which he so excelled.

**Stewart was the first** *racing driver to make serious money, while campaigning relentlessly for greater safety. The likeable Scot prepares to return to F1 full-time as proprietor of his own Ford-powered Grand Prix team in 1997.*

# NIGEL MANSELL
## MIXED EMOTIONS

**T**HERE IS A SAYING IN THE F1 PADDOCK that those who adored Nigel Mansell were the people who had never met him. That harsh exaggeration highlighted the feelings of some insiders towards a man bullish with self-confidence yet racked with wearying self-doubt.

Mansell would stand on the gas and wring every ounce of speed from a car, racing wheel-to-wheel with the fiercest rival and exhibiting the tenacity that prompted the selective Italian fans – the *tifosi* – to bestow upon him the soubriquet Il Leone (The Lion) during his days with Ferrari. Yet take him from the cockpit, and while he might be ebullient with good humour, equally he might complain about perceived slights and see plots against him at every turn.

Mansell came up the hard way in racing, investing all his own money as he attempted to climb the greasy pole from the lower ranks. Few rated him, and it was not until 1985, on the 72nd attempt, that he succeeded in winning his first Grand Prix. Yet from that moment onwards he blossomed into arguably the most competitive Englishman ever to sit in a Formula One car – certainly the most aggressive. His 31 Grand Prix successes place him behind only arch-rivals Senna and Prost in the all-time rankings.

It was as easy to see why the fans loved him – with his bristling moustache and down-home manner – as it was to see why those who had to work with him sometimes found his persecution complex hard going. He fudged his career in F1 at the very hour of his World Championship triumph in 1992, but won the IndyCar Championship in America the following year, at his first attempt.

A curious ragbag of contradictions, he was a hugely determined driver, whose character shortcomings sometimes obscured his achievements. It says everything about him as a driver that he was the one Senna knew he could not intimidate.

*"I intend to drive a human bulldozer through anyone who is not positive about me"*

**Always blindingly quick** *in the car, but a curious mix out of it, Nigel Mansell was a spectacular racer; his 1992 championship was just reward for unceasing determination.*

# NIKI LAUDA

## TO HELL AND BACK

**N**IKI LAUDA PRESENTS MANY IMAGES to race fans the world over. He is the Man Who Came Back from the Dead, following his astonishing recovery from the fiery accident in the German Grand Prix in 1976 that nearly killed him. He is The Rat to those who remember the contretemps with fearless paratrooper David Purley during the Belgian Grand Prix the following year. He is a triple World Champion. The man who advises Ferrari. Lauda is all of these, and more.

Even Mansell displayed greater potential than Lauda in the nursery formulae, and when the buck-toothed Austrian bought himself an F1 drive with March most wrote him off. March's engineers barely listened when he told them that their car didn't work. Yet within two years he was impressing with BRM, and by 1974 he was winning races for Ferrari, the new hotshoe grabbing at Stewart's vacant crown. He lost the Championship that year through lack of experience, but won it conclusively in 1975. He was leading in 1976 before the accident at the daunting Nurburgring, and won it again when he came back in 1977.

While the press romanticized his remarkable recovery, Lauda remained the supreme pragmatist. He lost the 1976 crown when he pulled out of the last race, unable to see adequately in the terrible conditions. He retired abruptly in 1979, set up his own airline, LaudaAir, and returned in 1982. He started winning again, and beat Prost cannily to the Championship in 1984 before retiring for good the following season. Now he brings his unique brand of cynicism and analysis to bear as consultant to Ferrari, where he remains as outspoken as ever.

Ever since the fire at the Nurburgring Lauda has worn the scars without flinching, facing the new circumstances with the practicality and dark humour he

always brought to his racing. They conceal a razor-sharp mind – and the relentless determination that won him three titles and built him an airline against international opposition.

**Blunt, cynical and possessed** *of a dark sense of humour, Niki Lauda won races and championships on his own terms through a combination of speed and intellectual superiority.*

# GRAHAM HILL
## A NATIONAL INSTITUTION

**W**HEN GRAHAM HILL'S PLANE crashed on Arkley Golf Course on a foggy night in November 1975, a nation lost an institution who epitomized motor racing to the man in the street.

As Hill had taken off from Marseilles the future held great promise; to the intense relief of his friends he had finally hung up his helmet after a record 176 Grand Prix starts, 14 victories, and two World Championships. He was the only man to have won the Triple Crown – the World Championship, the Indianapolis 500, and the Le Mans 24 Hour race. He was moulding his own F1 team around the prodigious talents of upcoming Tony Brise, who had just been shaking down their new car at the Paul Ricard circuit in southern France. Now all that remained for Hill's wife Bette, son Damon and daughters Brigitte and Samantha, were memories and a wealth of insurance claims from the families of team members, Brise among them, who had perished with him.

Norman Graham Hill did not start driving until he was 24 years old, but his determination and good humour opened doors. By 1962 he was ready for the World Championship with BRM. Six years later, with Jim Clark dead, Hill approached his 40th birthday by carrying the shattered Lotus team through its darkest days, and that year he won his second title against strong opposition from his former team-mate Jackie Stewart. A year later his career almost ended when he smashed both legs after being hurled from his car in the American Grand Prix, but he stunned doctors with the speed of his recovery and won a Championship point on his return in 1970. His son Damon has inherited the family trait of raising his game in deepest adversity.

With his flowing locks and Errol Flynn moustache Graham Hill was the life and soul of any party. A man who was always active, full of boundless energy, he was capable of exchanging jokes with the best comedians – and appeared on TV as the perfect foil for comedians Morecambe & Wise. When he died, even people who had never met him wept.

**Like Senna and Prost** *in the 1980s, Clark and Hill were the class of Formula One in the 1960s, each winning two World Championships. In that gentler era, however, both were firm friends off the race track, and had immense respect for one another when they were on it.*

# JOHN SURTEES
## PLOUGHING A LONELY FURROW

In **1964,** *in this Ferrari, John Surtees became World Champion on four wheels as well as two.*

**N**O MAN IS EVER LIKELY to emulate John Surtees' feat of winning World Championships on two wheels and four. A racer who would be equally at home in the Halls of Fame of both motor-cycle and car racing, 'Big John' rarely won the accolades his success deserved, for he was a man who kept his own counsel and ploughed his own furrow. His critics suggested that was his biggest problem.

He showed prodigious speed when he graduated to F1 with Lotus, before Colin Chapman forged his deep alliance with Jim Clark, but moved to pastures new just as the team came good. After winning the World Championship in a dramatic Mexican Grand Prix in 1964, he quit Ferrari in the middle of the 1966 season after internal pressure became intolerable, and thus left Jack Brabham a clear run to the title. After a dismal 1969 season he left BRM to set up his own team for 1970, just as BRM started winning again.

In a car, as on a bike, Surtees was a fearless but scrupulously fair competitor, but where most of his rivals contented themselves with riding or driving, he had a deep interest in the workings of his machines. Some said he should have concentrated solely on racing, itself difficult enough, but he liked to tinker and probe in an unceasing quest for technical perfection.

Surtees has few regrets, however. Such an approach worked perfectly well

*"Whatever happened there, I wouldn't have missed my time at Maranello"*

as his exploits on motor cycles passed into legend and he took MV Agusta to countless victories and the World Championships in 1956 (500 cc class), 1958, 1959 and 1960 (350 and 500). In that final year he also began the car-racing career that would take him to the unique double by the age of 30. A year after his Championship he was badly injured when his CanAm Lola crashed at Mosport Park in Canada, yet he astonished doctors with the speed of his recovery. Resilience was always Big John's strong suit.

# TECHNICAL

ONE OF THE MOST SIGNIFICANT PARTS OF ANY RACE team's annual budget is the cost of engines, which is why the majority seek agreements with major manufacturers in which the manufacturer supplies his engines free of charge and backs that with technical support.

Ferrari builds its own powerplants exclusively for its own use, while Renault supplies units to both Williams and Benetton. McLaren has an agreement with Mercedes-Benz, Jordan with Peugeot and Sauber with Ford. Tyrrell uses the Japanese Yamaha, while Ligier makes a financial contribution for its Mugen-Honda V10s, as Arrows does with Brian Hart's V8. With the demise of the Larrousse, Simtek and Pacific teams in recent years, Minardi and Forti are the only teams which now lease engines from Cosworth Engineering, which builds the Ford ED and Zetec-R V8s.

While proprietary suppliers have recognized tariffs (around £3.5m), major manufacturers are traditionally cagey about the cost of their investment, and release few financial details. Power and weight figures, as well as technical details such as bore and stroke measurements, are these days also closely guarded secrets. As an example, however, Ford's involvement with Sauber is thought to be worth around £10m per year; Renault and Mercedes-Benz may outspend that by at least a factor of two.

*The heart of the modern racing car is the engine. It is purpose-built and restricted to a maximum displacement of 3000cc – 3 litres. The engine is a critical part of the car, since it influences shape and weight distribution. The majority are thus V10s and Renault's, as shown here, is the yardstick.*

## WHAT IS AN F1 CAR WORTH?

**REAR WING:** *Highly popular site, especially on television. Around £5m.*

**ENGINE COVER:** *Very popular, very visible – and very expensive. Upwards of £10m.*

**SIDEPODS:** *Side panels are very popular and are worth upwards of £5m; tops can be part of the front-wing package – £3m+.*

**COCKPIT SIDES**: *Useful in television close-ups – £5m and over.*

WITH THE TOP TEAMS SUCH AS FERRARI, McLAREN AND WILLIAMS rumoured to be spending well over £50m annually, over and above the allowances for their free engine and Goodyear tyre supply deals, it's easy to see why sponsorship in motor racing is so crucial, and why it costs a great deal to get involved. Conversely, with massive global television exposure, it's also easy to see why so many multinational companies see value in creating the right image via the sport. But what are the individual parts of a racing car really worth? Value depends on how well a team has performed the previous year, and rates differ depending on television airtime 'won', but here are some ballpark figures for an upper-midfield team.

**NOSE**: *A natural area of great value – £5m and over.*

**FRONT WING**: *Less popular, but still worth £3m or more.*

# THE TEAMS

## FERRARI

SCUDERIA FERRARI, VIA ASCARI 55/57
41053 MARANELLO, MODENA, ITALY
TEL: 39 536 949111; FAX: 39 536 946488

*Entered F1:* 1950
*First victory:* 1951 (British GP)
*No. victories:* 105
*Championships:* 1952 D; 1953 D; 1956 D;
1958 D; 1961 D/C; 1964 D/C; 1975 D/C; 1976 C;
1977 D/C; 1979 D/C; 1982 C; 1983 C
*Team principal:* Luca di Montezemolo
*Technical director:* John Barnard
*Primary sponsors:* Marlboro and Fiat
*Engine:* Ferrari V10

D = World Drivers' Championship
C = World Constructors' Championship

**Ferrari brings class** *and character to the F1 pit lane, not to mention the engineering genius of John Barnard (inset).*

FERRARI IS THE GREATEST TEAM IN motorsport, and the longest established in Formula One, with an unbroken record of competition since the inauguration of the official World Championship in 1950. It is also the most successful statistically, with 105 Grand Prix victories to McLaren's 104, nine Drivers' World Championships (equal with McLaren) and eight Constructors' titles (one better than McLaren and Williams).

Ever since the late Enzo Ferrari, who died in 1988, 'borrowed' the Prancing Horse logo of First World War fighter ace Francesco Baracca and mounted it on the yellow shield of Modena, Ferrari has been a legend. The Italian fans, the *tifosi*, support it with the reverence and fervour Britons reserve for Manchester United. Ferrari is by far the best-funded team in recent years, and as such has come in for plentiful criticism for its poor results (its last championship was back in 1983), but despite periodical forecasts that Fiat will not keep investing money indefinitely, the great team continues. This year, with the combined talents of Michael Schumacher and legendary design guru John Barnard who, among other things, pioneered the use of carbon fibre for chassis construction, greatness is expected.

Could F1 survive without Ferrari? Of course it could, since it has kept going without other past greats such as Alfa-Romeo, Maserati, Cooper and Lotus. But it would never be the same. Somehow, for all its faults and foibles, Ferrari epitomizes not only the turbulence and passion of Grand Prix racing, but also its charisma, romance and spirit.

# TYRRELL

**A born survivor,** *the once great Tyrrell team has seen good days and bad in the last decade, but always comes back for more.*

TYRRELL'S GREATEST DAYS MAY WELL lie in the past, but this is a team that knows all about survival in a cruel and unsentimental world, and which periodically gives glimpses of its old potential from the halcyon days when Jackie Stewart was its king. Twice in recent history, in 1988 and again in 1993, it has come close to the edge, yet each time the design pragmatism of Harvey Postlethwaite, the former Hesketh and Ferrari engineer, has created a cornerstone for impressive recovery. Postlethwaite's 019 design of 1990 spearheaded the move to high noses with low-slung front wings.

In Ken Tyrrell the team has a figurehead who is a graduate of the school of hard knocks, one of the most bombastic figures in the paddock, but also one of the best-loved. This was the man who created the first Tyrrell in complete secrecy before displaying it to a stunned media, and the man who did the same thing when announcing his six-wheeled car in 1975. Tyrrell was once unexpectedly confronted with a plane-load of journalists while he was bound for Paris to complete a secret engine supply deal with Renault. Caught red-handed, he came clean, told them the truth, and was highly amused when not one of them chose to believe him! Assuredly, he is a dangerous man in a poker game.

After a series of very impressive performances in 1994 Tyrrell disappointed in 1995, but is set to bounce back again this season.

**TYRRELL RACING ORGANISATION LTD LONG REACH, OCKHAM, WOKING, SURREY GU23 6PE, ENGLAND TEL: 44 (0)1483 284955 FAX: 44 (0)1483 284892**

*Entered F1:* 1968
*First victory:* 1968 (Dutch GP)
*No. victories:* 23
*Championships:* 1971 D/C, 1973 D
*Team principal:* Ken Tyrrell
*Managing director, technical:* Harvey Postlethwaite
*Primary sponsor:* –
*Engine:* Yamaha V10

# WILLIAMS

**WILLIAMS GRAND PRIX ENGINEERING LTD
GROVE, WANTAGE
OXFORDSHIRE OX12 0DQ, ENGLAND
TEL: 44 (0)1235 777700
FAX: 44 (0)1235 764705**

*Entered F1:* 1970
*First victory:* 1979 (British GP)
*No. victories:* 83
*Championships:* 1980 D/C; 1981 C; 1982 D;
1986 C; 1987 D/C; 1992 D/C; 1993 D/C; 1994 C
*Team principal:* Frank Williams
*Technical director:* Patrick Head
*Chief designer:* Adrian Newey
*Primary sponsor:* Rothmans/Renault
*Engine:* Renault V10

EVERY NEW TEAM THAT HAS scraped its way into F1 has, at some time or another, comforted itself with the knowledge that Frank Williams's organization was once the butt of pit-lane jokes.

When his own inability to co-ordinate steering-wheel inputs with throttle control more often than not pitched him off the road, Williams finally realized that he was not cut out to be a racing driver, and began concentrating on running other people. By 1970 he was ready to go F1, with his friend Piers Courage driving a car built by de Tomaso. The combination held promise, but when Piers was killed in the Dutch GP, the enterprise almost foundered. For years Williams struggled on, running proprietary chassis and then his own machines near the back of the grid, until in 1976 he fell out with wealthy Austrian Walter Wolf, who had taken over the team, and was thrown out. Williams is a determined fellow, and with Patrick Head as his designer he obtained Saudi Arabian money and built a new team for 1977. By 1979 they were knocking on the door, and in 1980 Alan Jones won the team its first World Championship.

Since then Williams has endured a roadcar accident in 1986 that left him wheelchair-bound, the usual knocks of racing, and the death of Ayrton Senna at Imola in 1994, and along the way his team has established a reputation for excellence that is second to none.

**Frank Williams** *(above) is a survivor who has moulded his team into a winning entity renowned for its engineering excellence.*

# McLAREN

**B**UT FOR A COLLISION WITH JEAN-Louis Schlesser which put Ayrton Senna off the road during the 1988 Italian Grand Prix, McLaren would have completed the almost impossible feat of winning every race in an F1 season.

That year, more than any, typified the Woking team's approach, as Senna and Alain Prost used their turbocharged Honda-engined cars to humiliate their opposition. Their crushing successes brought criticism and invective, but the simple truth was that McLaren was the only team to have done its homework properly, and it was doing a far better job than anyone else. Right through until 1991 the red-and-white steamroller proved the class of the field, until Williams and Renault began to get its act together with the FW14 series of cars that year. Since then things have been rather different for the team which Bruce McLaren established as an F1 entity in 1966.

McLaren was an immensely popular New Zealander who engineered cars as well as he drove them. He was killed in 1970, but four years later Emerson Fittipaldi won the team its first Championship, and James Hunt repeated the triumph two years later. In 1980, however, sponsor Marlboro installed Ron Dennis as manager and John Barnard as designer after fortunes had slumped, and by the mid-1980s they had engineered a brilliant recovery which won championships for Niki Lauda, Prost and Senna. Since the withdrawal of Honda in 1992 McLaren has struggled, but it is honing its new partnership with Mercedes-Benz and after a trying 1995 is making progress again. Despite its problems, it remains one of the top teams.

**Efficient in the pits,** *McLaren is at an engineering crossroads. Neil Oatley and Prost (inset) must make the right decisions in 1996.*

**McLAREN INTERNATIONAL LTD**
**WOKING BUSINESS PARK**
**ALBERT DRIVE, WOKING**
**SURREY GU21 5JY, ENGLAND**
**TEL: 44 (0)1483 728211**
**FAX: 44 (0)1483 720157**

*Entered F1:* 1966
*First victory:* 1968 (Belgian GP)
*No. victories:* 104
*Championships:* 1974 D/C; 1976 D; 1984 D/C; 1985 D/C; 1986 D; 1988 D/C; 1989 D/C; 1990 D/C; 1991 D/C
*Team principals:* Ron Dennis/ Mansour Ojjeh
*Technical directors:* Neil Oatley/Alain Prost
*Primary sponsor:* Marlboro/Mercedes-Benz
*Engine:* Mercedes-Benz V10

# ARROWS

**A**RROWS IS THE LONGEST-SURVIVING team never to have won a Grand Prix, an uneasy accolade to bear. Yet some say it would almost be an embarrassment to team principals if it did, since they would have to raise their game and gear everything up another notch.

**ARROWS GRAND PRIX INTERNATIONAL LTD**
**39 BARTON ROAD, WATER EATON**
**INDUSTRIAL ESTATE**
**BLETCHLEY, MILTON KEYNES MK2 3HW,**
**ENGLAND**
**TEL: 44 (0)1908 270047**
**FAX: 44 (0)1908 274123**

*Entered F1:* 1978
*No. victories:* 0
*Team principals:* Jack Oliver/Alan Rees
*Technical director:* Alan Jenkins (designed 1996 car before joining Stewart Grand Prix)
*Engine:* Hart V8 or V10

Arrows evolved in 1978 when Jack Oliver and Alan Rees had a disagreement with Shadow team-owner Don Nichols, and set up their own equipe with Shadow designer Tony Southgate. Unfortunately, their first car bore rather too close a resemblance to the existing Shadow, and they were legally obliged to build another at very short notice. Getting over that controversy, Oliver and Rees settled down to establish a team that forged a reputation for efficient design and operation, but one which rarely looked like bringing home the goods. Nevertheless, they were happy with a top five place in the Constructors' ratings for many years, making a good living from their efforts. More recently, as teams such as Lotus, Larrousse, Simtek and Pacific have succumbed to the financial rigours of the sport, Oliver and Rees's

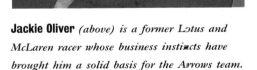

**Jackie Oliver** *(above) is a former Lotus and McLaren racer whose business instincts have brought him a solid basis for the Arrows team.*

genius at running a tight ship and knowing their limitations has really paid off.

Like Tyrrell, Arrows is a survivor. In Alan Jenkins it had a designer capable of producing extremely good cars, and in Brian Hart a man who can work technological wonders with his engines on the sort of budget that would barely keep Renault in coffee and croissants. With a little better funding, better fortune, and talents such as Verstappen's, Arrows could spring the odd surprise.

# JORDAN

**JORDAN GRAND PRIX LTD
BUCKINGHAM ROAD, SILVERSTONE
NORTHANTS NN12 8TN, ENGLAND
TEL: 44 (0)1327 857153
FAX: 44 (0)1327 857120**

*Entered F1:* 1991
*No. Victories:* 0
*Championships:* British F3 (87);
European F3000 (89)
*Team principal:* Eddie Jordan
*Technical director:* Gary Anderson
*Primary sponsor:* Benson & Hedges
*Engine:* Peugeot V10

**S**CEPTICISM GREETED EDDIE JORdan's boastful claims in 1989 that he was going to graduate to F1, even though he had already established an enviable reputation by winning the British F3 Championship in 1987 and the European F3000 series two years later. With the benefit of hindsight, as teams such as Coloni, Osella, Fondmetal, Dallara, Onyx, Lambo, Brabham, Lotus, Larrousse, Simtek and Pacific have all fallen by the wayside, it is now possible to assess just what Jordan has achieved since making his upward move in 1991. With what can now be seen as great shrewdness, but which at the time was regarded with

further scepticism, Jordan hired Gary Anderson to produce an extremely good-handling chassis and to look after the engineering side of the business, while he himself concentrated on making sure that the financial base was as strong as possible. In 1992 budgetary circumstance forced him to accept free Yamaha engines, and almost led to his downfall when the Japanese V12s proved uncompetitive, but after regrouping for 1993 around Brian Hart's neat V10 he pulled the team out of its technological dive. By 1994 Rubens Barrichello and Eddie Irvine were regularly qualifying strongly and pushing hard for championship points, and such progress finally attracted what Jordan coveted most of all: an in-depth relationship with an engine manufacturer. With Peugeot aboard, he further consolidated his position during 1995.

Now Jordan is pushing very hard to join the Top Four, leaving the sceptics wordless – and his supporters expectant. He is all too aware that he must win.

**Regarded as the team** *most likely to challenge the Top Four, Jordan must win at least one race in 1996.*

# LIGIER

**LIGIER SPORT**
**TECHNOPOLE DE LA NIEVRE**
**58470 MAGNY-COURS, FRANCE**
TEL: 33 86606200
FAX: 33 86212296/606297

*Entered F1:* 1976
*First victory:* 1977 (Swedish GP)
*No. victories:* 8
*Championships:* 0
*Team principals:* Briatore/Tom Walkinshaw
*Technical director:* Frank Dernie
*Primary sponsor:* Gitanes/Loto
*Engine:* Mugen-Honda V10

**O**NCE BILLED AS THE ONLY FRENCH racing team, Ligier is in danger of losing its identity now that it has been bought from Guy Ligier by principal shareholder Flavio Briatore and Tom Walkinshaw, the men who took Benetton to its current position of dominance. It remains based in France, at Magny-Cours, but there are plans for a new technical centre to take responsibility for design to be set up in England in the not too distant future.

Ligier entered F1 in 1976 using the Matra V12 engine, and over the years has employed a number of different makes of powerplant, ranging from Renault V6 and V10 to today's Mugen-Honda V10. Its most successful period was in 1979 and 1980, when its JS9 and JS10 chassis fought for championship supremacy with Williams and Ferrari.

The team was surrounded in a degree of controversy in 1995 when its JS41 bore an uncanny resemblance to Benetton's B195, something which Walkinshaw explained when he said: 'When you are conducting aerodynamic research into one concept, it makes sense to share it over two teams.' This is permissible under the regulations, and there were sufficient other detail differences to differentiate the two makes of car as far as the FIA was concerned. Though Ligier has stagnated in the past few years, Walkinshaw is committed to pushing it back into the Top Five.

**Under the leadership** *of Scot Tom Walkinshaw (below), the Ligier team (seen, bottom, at Monaco last season) has regained lost direction.*

# BENETTON

**Nobody matches Benetton's** *brilliance in the pits, where many of its races have been won.*

**B**ENETTON, THE REIGNING WORLD Champion constructor, was born out of the old Toleman team which entered F1 in 1981. Bucking established contemporary trends, Toleman ran a brace of ambitious turbocharged Hart-powered cars, an indication of its maverick nature that has somehow continued within Benetton.

The Italian clothing chain appeared in F1 as the sponsor of Tyrrell in 1982, before switching to Alfa Romeo in 1984. When Toleman ran into difficulties at the end of 1985, Benetton bought its assets and for 1986 put its name on the cars' badges as well as their sides. That year it scored its first victory, courtesy of Berger in Mexico.

In the ensuing years Benetton's threat developed steadily under the guidance of experienced former Lotus and Williams team manager Peter Collins, before current chief Flavio Briatore arrived to stir things up in 1989. A self-confessed businessman rather than racer, the controversial and colourful Briatore has forged hard-hitting deals with Ford, then Renault, and was instrumental in 'stealing' Michael Schumacher from Jordan after his début race in 1991. They grew in stature together, until their collaboration culminated in the German winning a controversial and incident-plagued World Championship in 1994. In 1995 Benetton added its first Constructors' title.

In the past Benetton has frequently been accused of running what is effectively a single-car team, concentrating all its efforts on Schumacher's requirements. In 1996 it must learn again how to give parity of equipment and attention to both drivers – Jean Alesi and the returning Gerhard Berger – now that the star it helped to create has departed for Ferrari.

**BENETTON FORMULA LTD**
**WHITEWAYS TECHNICAL CENTRE**
**ENSTONE, CHIPPING NORTON**
**OXFORDSHIRE OX7 4EE, ENGLAND**
**TEL: 44 (0)1608 678000**
**FAX: 44 (0)1608 678800**

*Entered F1:* 1986 (formerly Toleman)
*First victory:* 1986 (Mexican GP)
*No. victories:* 26
*Championships:* 1994 D; 1995 D/C
*Team principals:* Flavio Briatore/
Luciano Benetton/Alessandro Benetton
*Technical director:* Ross Brawn
*Research and development:* Rory Byrne
*Primary sponsor:* Mild Seven
*Engine:* Renault V10

# SAUBER

**TEAM SAUBER FORMEL 1**
**WILDBACHSTR 9**
**8340 HINWIL, SWITZERLAND**
**TEL: 41 1938 1400**
**FAX: 41 1938 1670**

*Entered F1:* 1993
*No. victories:* 0
*Championships:* World Sportscars (89 and 91)
*Team principal:* Peter Sauber
*Technical director:* Leo Ress
*Primary sponsor:* Red Bull/Petronas
*Engine:* Ford V10

FEW TEAMS HAVE BEEN PRIVILEGED enough to start their F1 life with as large a silver spoon in their mouths as Sauber, whose graduation from sportscars was masterminded and financed by Mercedes-Benz. Peter Sauber had established the most competitive team ever to come out of Switzerland when the Stuttgart manufacturer joined forces to compete in sportscar events, and following impressive triumphs at Le Mans and in the Championship itself, against heavy opposition from Mercedes' long-time rival Jaguar, both felt ready to move up. Mercedes was also responsible for financing the team's impressive new headquarters at Hinwil, which are as imposing as McLaren and Benetton's premises and are the envy of many smaller outfits.

Sauber's first season in 1993 showed strong promise, but 1994 was largely stagnant and did not bring the progress that had been expected. This prompted Mercedes to turn its allegiance instead to McLaren. Sauber, however, forged a fresh partnership with Ford. Though 1995 got off

**Aware that** *Jackie Stewart will take over as Ford's works team in 1997, and that Heinz-Harald Frentzen is being wooed by top teams, Peter Sauber faces a challenging season.*

to a difficult start, the C14 improved steadily throughout the year and the lead driver, Heinz-Harald Frentzen, was always a strong contender. In the final race of the year, in Adelaide, he ran a strong second for some time.

This year the German is partnered by two-time winner Johnny Herbert, and both will benefit from Ford's brand-new V10 Zetec-R powerplant. This will prove a crucial season for a team that can rightly be regarded as a top six contender, especially as Ford has already announced its partnership with Jackie Stewart for 1997.

# MINARDI

**MINARDI SCUDERIA ITALIA**
**MINARDI TEAM S.P.A.**
**VIA SPALLANZANI 21, 48018 FAENZA**
**RAVENNA, ITALY**
**TEL: 39 546 620480**
**FAX: 39 546 620998**

*Entered F1:* 1985
*No. victories:* 0
*Team principal:* Giancarlo Minardi
*Technical directors:* Mauro Gennari/
Gabriele Tredozi
*Primary sponsor:* –
*Engine:* Ford V8

**M**INARDI IS EVERYBODY'S FAVOURITE team. Well, almost. Big business shouldered Giancarlo Minardi aside in 1994 when he thought he had secured works Mugen-Honda engines. When he protested during 1995 he found bailiffs impounding his cars in France, home of the Ligier team which had won the Mugen-Honda deal. It was just another reminder of how tough F1 can be, and that it is better just to get on with things as best you can when you are a small team, rather than kicking against the traces.

Its 1995 chassis was one of the best, but Minardi lacks horsepower and money.

**Giancarlo Minardi's** *cars are always well designed and well turned out.*

# FORTI

**F**ORTI'S ENTRY INTO F1 IN 1995 WAS A marketing *tour de force*. Italian F3000 team owner Guido Forti had long aspired to emulate former rival Eddie Jordan and make the final big step to the top of the motorsport ladder, and when Carlo Gancia came seeking to further the interests of the Diniz family, and to establish a team in which Pedro Diniz could learn the ropes, Forti's dream came true.

Diniz's father owns a huge supermarket chain in South America and 'obliged' large client companies to back his plans; now that Pedro has moved to Ligier it remains to be seen how well Forti fares.

**Forti graduated to F1** *in 1995 courtesy of Pedro Diniz's money; it remains to be seen if it can survive without his backing in 1996.*

**FORTI GRAND PRIX**
**FORTI CORSE SRL, VIA EINUDI 33**
**ALESSANDRIA 115100, ITALY**
**TEL: 39 131 246890**
**FAX: 39 131 246891**

*Entered F1:* 1995
*No. victories:* 0
*Team principals:* Guido Forti/Carlo Gancia
*Technical director:* Giorgio Stirano
*Primary sponsor:* Parmalat
*Engine:* Ford Zetec R V8

# INDEX